ENCOUNTER THE
3D BIBLE

HOW TO READ THE BIBLE SO IT COMES TO LIFE

Dr. Susan Michael

Encounter the 3D Bible: How to Read the Bible So It Comes to Life
by Susan M. Michael

Email: embassy.publishers@icejusa.org
Web: www.embassypublishers.org

Copyright © 2022 Susan Michael

Embassy Publishers
PO Box 332974
Murfreesboro, TN 37133-2974

All rights reserved. No part of this book may be reproduced in any form, stored in a retrieval system, or transmitted in any form by any means—electronic, mechanical, photocopy, recording, or otherwise—without permission from the publisher, except as permitted by US copyright law.

Unless otherwise indicated, all Scripture quotations are from the New King James Version®. Copyright © 1982 by Thomas Nelson. Used by permission. All rights reserved.

Scripture quotations marked (NIV) are taken from the *Holy Bible*, New International Version®, NIV®. Copyright © 1973, 1978, 1984, 2011 by Biblica, Inc.™ Used by permission of Zondervan. All rights reserved worldwide. www.zondervan.com. The "NIV" and "New International Version" are trademarks registered in the United States Patent and Trademark Office by Biblica, Inc.™

Scripture quotations marked (ESV) are from *The ESV® Bible* (the *Holy Bible*, English Standard Version®), copyright © 2001 by Crossway, a publishing ministry of Good News Publishers. Used by permission. All rights reserved.

Scripture quotations marked (NLT) are taken from the *Holy Bible*, New Living Translation, copyright ©1996, 2004, 2015 by Tyndale House Foundation. Used by permission of Tyndale House Publishers, Carol Stream, Illinois 60188. All rights reserved.

Print ISBN: 978-0-9839374-3-2
Digital ISBN: 978-0-9839374-6-3
For permissions contact: embassy.publishers@icejusa.org

Editorial: Susan Michael, Tricia Miller; Copyeditor: Karen Engle
Cover design and layout: Peter Ecenroad
Formatting: Nancy Schimp

Printed in the United States of America.

— PRAISE FOR —
ENCOUNTER THE 3D BIBLE

One question a pastor or spiritual leader will inevitably encounter is, "Where do I begin so that I can grow to truly understand my Bible?" It's an honest admission that across 1,189 chapters, the countless strangely named people and places can be daunting to any "would-be" Bible student. Here Susan Michael guides our feet back to the beginning and sketches out the "first steps" to help us begin proper Bible study. Even more, this book offers important guidelines and considerations we can use to continuously check whether we are, in fact, understanding the Bible properly as we open its pages throughout our lifetime. It is worth your time and attention because it can help you unlock the keys to understanding the very words of the God who created you!

Dr. Randall D. Smith, *International Director*
CHRISTIAN TRAVEL STUDY PROGRAMS, INC.

I've learned so much from Susan Michael over the years. I've read her articles in magazines and newsletters and personally experienced her teachings on Israel study tours as well as in conferences and seminars. But Susan really "outdid herself" with this new book. I've graduated Bible college, been a pastor and Bible teacher for nearly 40 years, and personally led about 16 study tours to Israel—yet I've never read a more comprehensive and yet easy-to-read book explaining the Bible itself than *Encounter the 3D Bible*. I wish I had read this book when I was in Bible college.

If you really want to understand the Bible, read *Encounter the 3D Bible* right away. It will probably be the best single book you'll ever read on the subject, and what you learn will benefit you for years to come.

Jerry Dirmann, *Founding Pastor* of
**THE ROCK (FOURSQUARE CHURCH) NETWORK
and SOLID LIVES HOUSE CHURCHES**

Dr. Susan Michael's new book sets the standard for understanding Israel's place and purpose within the Word of God. It will serve as an excellent teaching tool for the church and a strong refutation of the widespread Replacement Theology heresy being taught today. Susan's easy-to-read and understandable teaching style and her vast knowledge and involvement with Israel, coupled with her extensive experience as the director of the International Christian Embassy Jerusalem (ICEJ), United States Branch, makes *Encounter the 3D Bible* a must-read for the body of Christ.

Dr. H. Dean Haun, *Senior Pastor*
FIRST BAPTIST CHURCH, Morristown, TN
and *President/Founder*
HARVEST OF ISRAEL and HARVEST OF ISRAEL TOURS

Have you had trouble getting into the Bible? Does it seem that the overall message gets lost in its thousands of details? Have you wondered if there is an easy-to-understand book that gives you the basic teaching of the Bible? And one that explains how to understand Israel and the Old Testament? This book is for you. It will help the Bible move from 2D to 3D. It is perfect for a Sunday School class or Bible study group.

Rev. Dr. Gerald McDermott, *Retired Anglican Chair of Divinity*
SAMFORD UNIVERSITY BEESON DIVINITY SCHOOL
Birmingham, AL

All serious believers read the Bible, but many lack the valuable principles, background, and tools needed to maximize the experience. Susan Michael provides a very readable, balanced, and understandable book full of wise guidance, so Bible reading need not be a confusing, mechanical chore but an inspiring success. I enthusiastically recommend this book.

Marvin R. Wilson, *H. J. Ockenga Professor Emeritus*
DEPARTMENT OF BIBLICAL STUDIES, GORDON COLLEGE
Wenham, MA

It is exciting to read a book that takes the black and white of the Bible and brings it to a three-dimensional level of understanding. Dr. Susan Michael has done that. *Encounter the 3D Bible* is a book that all people should read, no matter where they are in their relationship with God. This "get-to-the-point" book tackles many tough questions about the Bible and gives us an easy-to-follow 3D road map to the answers. This is one of those books that you want to share with others, knowing they will enjoy it.

Cary Summers, *President Emeritus*
MUSEUM OF THE BIBLE
Washington, DC

Every Evangelical pastor should read this book! Dr Susan Michael has written a timely, concise, and theologically excellent book on the great story of God's relationship between the Jewish people, the covenant land of Israel, and the church. Get this book—read it, study it, pass it on to others!

Dr. Tony Crisp, PhD, *President*
TRUE LIFE CONCEPTS

—CONTENTS—

Foreword		viii
Acknowledgements		x
Introduction		xi
Chapter 1	Why Study the Bible?	13
Chapter 2	How to Read the Bible at the 3D Level	23
Chapter 3	The Story of the Bible	41
Chapter 4	How Should Christians Read the Old Testament?	61
Chapter 5	The Land of the Bible	75
Chapter 6	The People of the Bible	95
Chapter 7	The God of the Bible	111
Chapter 8	The Search Begins	125
Appendix A	Old Testament Timeline	133
Appendix B	Recommended Resources	134

— FOREWORD —

It's rare in life to sit across from someone you've never met and instantly know it is a God-ordained moment that will bond you for life as friends. Yet that's what happened when I met Susan Michael for the first time in 2007 while we were organizing a women's conference in Jerusalem. Susan and I were drawn to each other like magnets, and the reason is simple: We both love the Word of God, and we both love Israel. That common foundation has knitted us together for more than 15 years. And even though our lives, ministries, and callings kept us busy, for many years, Susan and I made sure to meet up for lunch at the annual National Religious Broadcasters conference to catch up and talk about what God was doing in our lives and ministries.

Through that friendship, I've witnessed Susan's passionate love for the Word of God and her deep desire for people to understand it for themselves. The Bible is truly a "lamp to [her] feet and a light to [her] path" (Psalm 119:105). She walks each day in the light of the Word of God, and it is reflected in everything she does.

I've been to Israel many times, have led numerous teaching tours there, and have written a historical novel, *Israel My Beloved.* The land of Israel and the city of Jerusalem feel like home to me, and the people of Israel are dear to my heart. *But Susan's background and experience regarding Israel are at another level.* This is a person who has been there more than 75 times over the last 45 years. She studied for two years in Jerusalem as a college student. She's led teaching tours for decades and spoken at conferences about Israel internationally. She is a leader of a global ministry headquartered in Jerusalem. Israel is practically in her blood. And it is reflected in the book you are about to read: *Encounter the 3D Bible.*

I love anything that is true to the Word of God, and *Encounter the 3D Bible* is just that. It's a unique and powerful resource for anyone who wants to understand the Bible—both the Old and New Testaments—and how every word, story, and event is knitted together perfectly. So many people want to read and study the Bible but don't know where to start. Or when they read it, they don't know how to connect the people and places in the stories and lose interest. Susan wrote this book to change that!

For Susan, the Bible is "the most exciting book on the planet." And she has penned this book in a way that I am confident will help any reader, regardless of age, biblical background, or preconceived ideas about the Bible, understand it better and approach it from the proper perspective.

Most importantly, I believe *Encounter the 3D Bible* is critical for the day and hour in which we live. Isaiah 59:14–15 (NASB) says: "Justice is turned back, and righteousness stands far away; for truth has stumbled in the street, and uprightness cannot enter. Truth is lacking." This describes the times and the culture we are living in so well! Righteous behavior is hard to find. Truth has stumbled in the streets. God's truth is disregarded. Even many churches are not teaching according to what the Word of God says, and people do not realize this because they do not have a true biblical perspective. Isaiah warns against this, saying that those who do not speak according to the "Law and the testimony ... have no dawn" (Isaiah 8:20). There is no light, no illumination, in them.

This is why Susan wrote this book. As she realized that more and more people were learning and believing distortions about the Bible and, specifically, the Old Testament, she couldn't let it rest. She realized the desperate need for a resource that would help everyone—not-yet-believers, new believers, and longtime students of the Word—know *how* to read and study the Bible so it comes to life. Susan writes in an easy-to-follow and down-to-earth way that spells everything out simply so that after reading this book, readers will have a firm foundation for how to read the Bible and discover God's truth for themselves.

Truth has indeed "stumbled in the streets" and is lacking in our day. But *Encounter the 3D Bible* can help turn the tide. I'm confident anyone who reads this book will be better able to interpret God's Word for themselves and rightly discern when they read or hear biblical interpretation *not* according to the Scriptures.

It's a book that should be on everyone's bookshelf—if not several on hand to give to others—and I am honored and delighted to recommend it.

Kay Arthur
Bible Teacher
Cofounder of Precept Ministries International
Four-Time ECPA Christian Book Award-Winning Author

— ACKNOWLEDGEMENTS —

My first word of thanks must go to Dr. Roy Hayden, retired professor of biblical studies at Oral Roberts University, for encouraging me to go on a study trip to Israel in 1978. That trip changed the trajectory of my life because of the way my Bible came alive, and it is the basis for *Encounter the 3D Bible*. However, I could have never gone on that trip had it not been for the support of my parents, Sam and Annie McElroy. Although my father believed strongly in the importance of education, it had to have been hard for them to allow their 19-year-old daughter to fly to Israel alone to study.

During my studies in Jerusalem and over the years since then, I have learned so much from so many people it is impossible to list them all. But I would be remiss not to mention the teachers and resources that stand out as ones that shaped and/or affirmed the approach to the Bible as presented in this book: Rev. Malcolm Hedding, Dr. Labib Mikhail, Dr. Jack Hayford, Dr. Gerald McDermott, Samuel Whitefield, Lois Tverberg, Dr. Marvin Wilson, Dr. Michael Brown, and Kay Arthur. I also want to acknowledge my good friend Rabbi Shmuel Bowman, a Torah scribe who is always happy to advise me on a Hebrew word or Jewish practice.

What started as podcast episodes have now been turned into this beautifully written book thanks to long hours of labor by the talented writer and editor Karen Engle. Dr. Tricia Miller brought her doctorate in Hebrew Bible and years of experience speaking in both synagogues and churches to help us fine-tune some of the points being made.

Dr. Marvin Wilson spent many hours combing through this manuscript. His long teaching career and pioneering role in Evangelical-Jewish relations made his assistance and direction invaluable to me. And I am incredibly grateful for another scholar and theologian, Dr. Gerald McDermott, who alerted me to the complexities of some of the theological issues I was trying to state in simple layperson's terms.

Finally, I want to thank my husband, George Michael, for his support and encouragement over three decades now. I have learned so much from him about the Middle East and gained from his perspective on events as an Egyptian Christian. His encouragement, which kept me going despite the many times I became discouraged, has brought me to this day and the accomplishment of this book. Thank you, Habibi.

— INTRODUCTION —

I was just 19 years old when I first had the opportunity to go to Israel on a summer study program, and it changed my life! Studying the Bible in its physical, cultural, and religious settings made it go from two-dimensional to three-dimensional. If you've never been to Israel, the land where the story of the Bible unfolded, perhaps one day you can go with me and experience the Bible in 3D for yourself.

In the meantime, may you encounter the Bible as never before through the pages of this book, where I offer insights, visual images, and information gleaned from four decades of traversing Israel. Along the way, I'll answer questions about the Bible, its story, and your own walk with the Lord.

When I hear people say that the Bible is hard to understand or that they don't know where to begin to study it—or worse yet, that they don't even believe it—my heart aches. For me, the Bible is the most exciting book on the planet. The story that began in Genesis is not over—it continues today, and we are privileged to be able to see our Bibles come alive as ancient prophecies are fulfilled.

Encounter the 3D Bible is not a Bible study but a journey into the world of the Bible. It will make every sermon and Bible study you participate in make more sense because you will understand the story behind the stories.

Together we will review the master story that began in eternity past. Along the way, I'll share insights and tips on how to read your Bible and why you can trust what is written in this amazing book. We'll explore why the Jewish people—who have returned to their ancient homeland and built a modern nation in our day—are living proof of God's existence, power, and faithfulness.

It will be a journey that will deepen your faith and walk with the Lord like none other. It may just change your life too.

Susan Michael,
ICEJ USA Director

CHAPTER ONE

Why Study the Bible?

I love Your commandments, more than gold.
—Psalm 119:127

Can you say along with the psalmist that you love God's commandments more than gold? That is quite a statement of how valuable and precious the Word of God is. Yet many people do not even attempt to read the Scriptures because they find the Bible hard to understand.

Others have been told the Bible is untrue and contains contradictions and errors. As a result, their minds are filled with doubt, just as the serpent filled Eve's mind with doubt in the garden of Eden when he questioned, "Did God *really* say?" The doubt in Eve's mind grew into disbelief and disobedience, resulting in sin and much suffering.

These lies are designed to mislead Christians from knowing the power and strength they will gain from spending time in the Word. The Bible is not only filled with insights for living a full and meaningful life, but it is inspired by the Holy Spirit—so time spent reading it is time spent in fellowship with God *through* the Holy Spirit. It is a unique book that tells a fascinating story but can also change lives.

It changed mine, and it can change yours.

My Bible came alive for me some 40 years ago when I had the privilege to study the Scriptures in their physical and historical setting—surrounded by the eastern culture and Jewish religion it speaks to—in Israel.

I was a biblical studies major in university at the time and had heard about people studying abroad during the summer. So I asked one of my professors if he knew of any study programs in Israel, to which he enthusiastically said, "Absolutely! And go, if possible, because it will change your life."

He was right.

THE ABCs OF READING THE BIBLE

Countless excellent resources are available that teach how to study the Bible. And though they are valuable for better equipping us to *interpret* God's Word, few teach us *how* to read the Bible. Just as a child must learn their ABCs before they can progress to reading words, sentences, and paragraphs, we, too, must learn the ABCs of how to read the Bible.

Unfortunately, most Bible study resources skip this beginning step, which involves three different levels of Bible reading: the inspirational level, the Bible study level, and the cultural/historical or "3D" level. Before addressing each in chapter 2, we must first establish the importance of studying the Bible in the first place. It could be the most important thing we do in our lives—it is that essential.

WHY STUDY THE BIBLE?

Perhaps you are thinking, *I go to church every Sunday. I listen to the sermon. Why do I need to study the Bible?*

Great question!

One way Jesus answered people's questions in the Bible was to respond with His own questions—so let me be "biblical" and do the same:

- Do you want to understand the universe and the purpose of life?
- Do you want to understand *your* purpose in life?

WHY STUDY THE BIBLE?

- Do you want to know God better?
- Do you want to have more of His power in your life?

Only the Bible contains the answers—and everything else you need to know to live your life. It's why the psalmist could say, "Your word is a lamp to my feet and a light to my path" (Psalm 119:105). But the Bible is more than an informative or instructional book. Yes, you will want to learn to study the Scriptures for this reason—but there are several others.

1. The Bible Is Powerful

The apostle Paul wrote in 2 Timothy 3:16, "All Scripture is given by inspiration of God." The Greek word for "inspiration" literally means "God-breathed." This means the words within the pages of your Bible are alive, active, and powerful. When you read them, you are fellowshipping with the Holy Spirit and making yourself available for God to work in your heart, speak to you about your life, and give you direction.

When I was 16 years old, I became curious about God and Christianity, so I asked the pastor of our church if there was a Bible written in a modern translation that was easier to read and understand. He recommended a new translation of the New Testament, and I promptly bought it. A few weeks later, a friend asked if I could fill in for her at work while she went on a two-week vacation. She worked at the local YMCA managing its small gym. All I had to do was help people use the equipment and ensure they used it properly and were safe. Few people used the gym, and if they did, it was only for about 10 minutes, so there really wasn't much for me to do.

I brought my New Testament to work, and over the next two weeks, I read the entire book, cover to cover. When I finished, there was a power at work in my life that had not been there before. I knew it. I felt it. I had a new inner resolve to follow the still, small voice nudging me as I had been reading.

That time I had spent in the pages of the Bible had infused my spirit with the power of the Holy Spirit. A few weeks later while attending a church service, I gave my life to the Lord, and I've never looked back.

2. The Bible Tends to the "Whole Person"

Growing spiritually is more important than many of us realize—that is, until we grasp the "whole person" concept. We find it in 1 Thessalonians 5:23 where Paul wrote:

> Now may the God of peace Himself sanctify you completely; and may your whole *spirit*, *soul*, and *body* be preserved blameless until the coming of the Lord Jesus Christ. (Emphasis added)

Paul referenced three things in this verse: "*spirit*, *soul*, and *body*." God created every person as a tri-part being made up of a spirit, a soul (our mind and emotions), and a body. And each needs to be cared for so that the person can be whole and healthy.

The Christian university I attended was built on the "whole person" concept found in this verse and had a well-rounded program that addressed all three parts of our being. Each day, while building our minds and intellect, we also had to build our physical well-being through exercise.

In addition, we had mandatory chapel services, worship services, and Bible studies that ensured we also strengthened and developed our spiritual life. Four years of repeatedly hearing about this concept of caring for spirit, soul, and body instilled in me a lifelong commitment to spiritual, mental, and physical health.

We know how to build physical strength (though it's sometimes hard to do it!), and we know how to increase our intellect. But how can we develop our spirit? One way is spending time in the Word of God, letting God's Spirit speak to us and direct us so we can go forth and live our lives in the power of the Spirit.

3. The Bible Is the Most Exciting Book on the Planet!

More than what we can gain from time spent in the Bible is the fact that it is simply an amazing book. It is in a league of its own—I call it "the most exciting book on the planet." What other book has 66 different books written by 40 different people over approximately 1,500 years that tell real-life stories that corroborate the nature and character of God? Where else can we read about events in the life of a nation that foreshadowed future events and demonstrated the consistent hand of God at work throughout history? What other book predicted events unfolding in our day and tells us what the future still holds?

Only the Bible.

The Bible is inspired by the Holy Spirit who speaks to us through its ancient words—some penned 3,500 years ago. The stories teach us about one God and contain prophecies coming to fulfillment *in our day*.

America is a mere 250 years old, which sounds like a long time—and 1,000 years seems like an eternity! Yet many of the things God spoke to Abraham almost 4,000 years ago are coming to fulfillment in this generation. It's truly the most exciting book on the planet!

ISRAEL—WHERE THE STORIES OF THE BIBLE TOOK PLACE

I take groups to Israel every year, and hopefully, you can join me one day. If you do, I'll take you to one of my favorite places: a 4,000-year-old gate made from mud bricks located in the far north of the country. The gate opens to the ancient city of Dan, known as Laish in Abraham's time.

The first book of the Bible, Genesis, references this city. Genesis 14:13–16 tells how the king of Elam and his allies abducted Abraham's nephew, Lot, and how Abraham went to the region near Laish (later called Dan) to rescue him. Abraham may have passed through that very gate—that's how old it is!

Every time I approach the gate, I pause and contemplate how profound it is that God has allowed us to see something so old. I think:

Our father Abraham probably walked right up these stairs and through that gate into that city.

The 4,000-year-old Abrahamic Gate in Tel Dan, Israel, one of the oldest—if not the oldest—remaining gates in the world (source: commons.wikimedia.org)

Many other exciting archaeological finds have confirmed the historicity of the biblical accounts. Traveling and studying in Israel, surrounded by fulfilled prophecy, helps people read the Bible at the 3D level. That's what happened when I went to Israel on that first study trip.

Though you may not be able to travel to Israel, this book will bring a little of Israel to you so that you can also start reading the Bible in 3D.

YOU CAN BELIEVE THE BIBLE

The authenticity of the Bible is under attack like never before. Perhaps you have encountered this and been told that the Bible is unreliable and untrue. However, you can be confident in the accuracy of this phenomenal book—and here are two key reasons why.

The Jewish Commitment to Accurate Preservation of the Law

We have the Jewish people to thank for passing down ancient manuscripts copiously written to perfection. Out of reverence for the Word of God, Jewish scribes were committed to extreme accuracy when recording and copying the text. When writing a new manuscript (scroll), if a scribe made a mistake, it invalidated the entire scroll, and if they could not correct it, they threw the whole manuscript away and started over from the beginning. One tiny error could change the meaning of a word—the very words of God—so scribes took extreme care to write every single letter perfectly.

The Discovery of the Dead Sea Scrolls

Proof of this accuracy was broadcast to the world with the groundbreaking discovery of the Dead Sea Scrolls in 1947. These scrolls are ancient Hebrew manuscripts found in the Qumran caves in the dry Judaean Desert. Scholars date these scrolls from the last three centuries BC to the first century AD. For 2,000 years those scrolls were protected in earthenware vessels (an ancient Jewish custom) in 12 different caves until

One of the Qumran caves in the Judaean Desert where the Dead Sea Scrolls were discovered

a Bedouin shepherd boy stumbled upon them in 1947.

Every book of the Hebrew Bible (our Old Testament) is represented in those scrolls except the book of Esther. Carbon testing dates some of the scrolls to about 200 years before the time of Jesus. Yet they closely match the manuscripts our translators have been working from to translate our Bibles, affirming their authenticity and giving us a high degree of confidence that the Bible we have today is accurate.

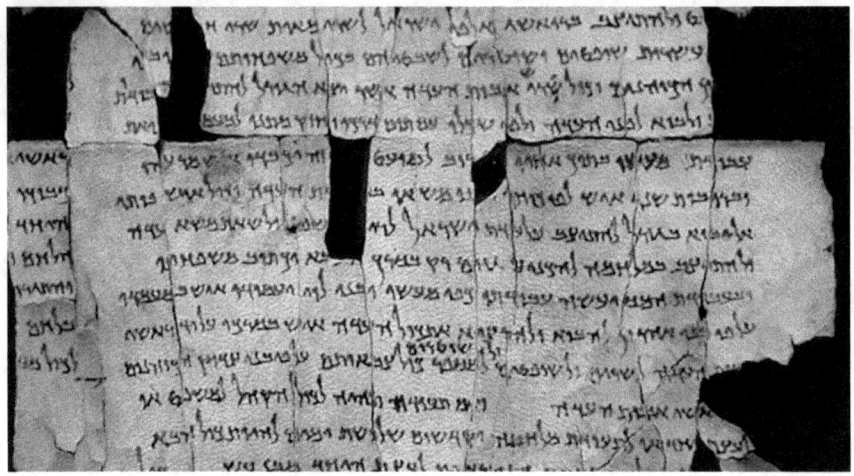

Part of Dead Sea Scroll 28a from Qumran Cave 1

THE VICTORIOUS WORD OF GOD

The Word of God is not just accurately transmitted, but it is true and powerful—which explains why the devil hates it and tries to draw us away from it:

> Now the serpent was more crafty than any of the wild animals the LORD God had made. He said to the woman, "Did God really say, 'You must not eat from any tree in the garden'?" The woman said to the serpent, "We may eat fruit from the trees in the garden, but God did say, 'You must not eat fruit from the tree that is in the middle of the garden, and you must not touch it, or you will die.'" (Genesis 3:1–3 NIV)

In this passage, the evil tempter, in the form of the serpent, approached Eve and asked her, "Did God *really* say that?" instilling doubt in Eve's mind. Eve nurtured that doubt, and soon she was unsure whether God meant what He said—if He said it at all. In Eve's mind, God must not have *really* meant it. So she ate from the tree, initiating the downward moral spiral of humanity.

Doubting God and His Word is not new. Many think that people today are much more enlightened and intellectual than past generations who "foolishly believed that the Bible was the Word of God." But there is nothing new about doubt. Today, just as he did with Adam and Eve, the tempter uses doubt—and other distractions, such as the media, earthly pleasures, the internet, fear, and worry (see 1 Peter 5:8)—to draw people away from the Word of God because he knows how powerful the truth of Scripture can be in their lives.

The last book of the Bible, Revelation, reveals the incredible and victorious power of the Word of God:

> I saw heaven standing open and there before me was a white horse, whose rider is called Faithful and True. With justice he judges and wages war. His eyes are like blazing fire, and on his head are many crowns. He has a name written on him that no one knows but he himself. He is dressed in a robe dipped in blood, and *his name is the Word of God*. The armies of heaven were following him, riding on white horses and dressed in fine linen, white and clean. Coming out of his mouth is a sharp sword with which to strike down the nations. "He will rule them with an iron scepter." He treads the winepress of the fury of the wrath of God Almighty. On his robe and on his thigh he has this name written: KING OF KINGS AND LORD OF LORDS. (Revelation 19:11–16 NIV, emphasis added)

John's vision in this passage is of the end of the story: Christ's return to

Earth on a white horse, victorious, and the rider's name is "the Word of God." The Bible begins in Genesis with the question: "Is that *really* what God said?" But it ends in Revelation with proof of the power of the Word of God and that God's promises are true.

Jesus is the Word of God made flesh. He is fully divine but also fully human. In the same way, the Bible is fully human—penned by human authors—yet Paul affirmed that every word was "given by inspiration of God" (2 Timothy 3:16) through the Holy Spirit. Therefore, the Bible is infused with the Holy Spirit, and because God's Spirit is alive, God's Word is alive too.

Jesus said in John 6:63 that the very words He spoke "are spirit, and they are life." Hebrews 11 tells us that the world was created and formed by God's spoken word.

The Bible is living and powerful—that's why we must spend time reading it, meditating on it, and letting it infuse our lives with His Spirit and power.

When we do, we will never be the same.

CHAPTER TWO

How to Read the Bible at the 3D Level

*I have not departed from your laws,
for you yourself have taught me.*
—Psalm 119:102 NIV

Essential to living the Christian life is studying the Bible at the devotional level—intending to apply what we learn to our daily lives. At this level we can read a story or a verse in the Bible and not understand its context but still take away a meaning or message for our life.

However, the danger of reading only at the personal, devotional level is that we can take Scripture out of context, which increases the possibility of misunderstanding and drawing wrong conclusions. Therefore, we should not stop at the devotional level but also study at a more intentional, doctrinal level and eventually at what I call the 3D level.

Don't get me wrong! No one level is incorrect; it is just incomplete. We should routinely read the Bible at all three levels. But in my experience, few people make it to the 3D level, and because of this, they miss out on understanding the Bible in its proper historical, cultural, and religious context. And that's where I can help—I'll connect the dots from

Genesis to Revelation and fill in those contextual gaps so that you may start to understand just how exciting the Bible and the story within its pages are.

So let's get started!

BEGIN WITH PRAYER

Always begin your time reading and studying the Bible with prayer. Prayer is simply talking with God—it's how the human soul that God created communicates with the One who created it. Ask God to help you understand His Word and use it to speak to your heart.

The apostle Paul was one of the most influential leaders of the early Christian church and was instrumental in spreading the gospel to many parts of the Roman Empire. About 25 percent of the New Testament consists of letters he wrote to those churches.

In one letter to the church at Ephesus, a city in ancient Greece (the western part of present-day Turkey), Paul said he prayed that God would give the Ephesian believers wisdom and revelation:

> Therefore I also, after I heard of your faith in the Lord Jesus and your love for all the saints, do not cease to give thanks for you, making mention of you in my prayers: that the God of our Lord Jesus Christ, the Father of glory, may give to you the spirit of wisdom and revelation in the knowledge of Him, the eyes of your understanding being enlightened. (Ephesians 1:15–18)

A good practice is asking God to give you wisdom and revelation as you spend time in His Word so, like the Ephesians, you may also have a greater understanding. Why? Because God is after a relationship with you. Head knowledge is good, beneficial, and informative, but God wants you to spend time with Him and in His Word so that what you learn will be more than mere facts.

Though books and sermons commentating on the Bible are not bad in and of themselves, there's something beautiful about reading and studying the Bible. World-renowned Bible teacher Kay Arthur often says we don't need secondhand knowledge—we need firsthand knowledge, which comes from studying the Bible for ourselves.

Through more intentional study, as the truths within its pages drop into your heart and spirit, knowledge about the Word of God will change from just head knowledge to personal revelation. It will be as though God is personally teaching you through the Holy Spirit.

WHERE TO START READING

After praying, it's time to dive in!

Many teachers encourage new Bible readers to start with the Gospels—especially the Gospel of John—and I agree. If you have more time, I encourage you to read the book of Proverbs too. Proverbs has 31 chapters, which means if you read a chapter a day, you will cycle through the entire book in a month. Proverbs is full of practical wisdom and great advice for living your life in a way that honors God.

You can also read out of the book of Psalms. There are 150 psalms, which will keep you busy for a while! You can read one or two psalms a day along with a proverb and a chapter from one of the Gospels, like John—a great combination to begin reading the Bible.

HOW TO READ THE BIBLE

More important than *where* to start reading the Bible, however, is *how* to read it. For example, you might finish reading John, Proverbs, or Psalms and glean some good information to apply to your life. But without knowing *how* to read it, you might come away with little understanding of the overarching message or context of the passage.

To better understand what you are reading, it's essential to dig into Scripture a little deeper. First, let's talk about the different ways to approach reading the Bible.

Level 1: Inspirational Level

Many people study the Bible at what I call "Level 1," the inspirational or personal application level. We tend to approach the Bible this way because we want an answer to the question, "What does the Bible say?" so we can apply it to our lives. Most sermons are also focused on personal application—and rightfully so because pastors want us to take the principles from the Bible and apply them to our lives.

When I first came to faith in Jesus and trusted Him as my Savior, I was just 16 going on 17. I knew nothing about the Bible, but as I began to read it, I loved it and saw it as my spiritual guidebook giving me direction for living a life pleasing to the Lord.

Bible teachers often tell people to read the Bible as though it's written to them personally, and that's what I did as a young believer—I read it to see how I should live my life. Often, verses would jump off the page into my heart! It was as though the Lord was using my Bible to speak to me intimately, giving personal affirmation or direction for my life.

However, reading the Bible only in this way can be dangerous because we can take a verse out of context and end up in error if we don't know the broader picture of what that verse was about originally. This doesn't mean we should stop reading the Bible for inspiration and personal application. It just means we should also begin to study it at a deeper level.

Level 2: Bible Study Level

The second level of study, a more theological or doctrinal level, is less about personal application and more about understanding the key doctrines about God, His character, and His ways. Studying at this level is essential for spiritual maturity and effectiveness in ministry to others. It might involve topical studies, whole book studies, or apologetics (how to answer questions and accusations against Christianity or the Bible).

I learned to study my Bible at a more theological level while at university, where I majored in biblical studies. *But you do not have to get a degree to study this way*—you can join Bible studies at your church or study the Bible alongside a plethora of online resources. (See Appendix B for resources I recommend.)

This level involves reading the Bible to learn about God—His character, His ways, and how He deals with His people—rather than for personal edification. It involves things like:

- Reading to understand key doctrines in the Bible, such as salvation, righteousness, and judgment
- Doing word studies to learn the meaning of terminology in the original language (Hebrew, Greek, or Aramaic)
- Doing topical studies to unpack details of specific events, people, or themes
- Digging deep into a book of the Bible, such as John or Galatians

While in university I still read my Bible on a devotional, personal level while I also studied the Bible in class to understand its doctrines. I made straight As in all my classes because I loved the subject so much.

However, none of that prepared me for what would happen when I went to Israel to study in the land where many of the stories of the Bible had taken place.

Level 3: The "3D" Level

In Israel I was surrounded by the Hebraic culture the Bible reflected, the Jewish people it was about, and ancient prophecies being fulfilled. I traced biblical events on maps, then visited the actual sites they described—and realized the Scriptures I read for inspiration were also a detailed historical account of events that had taken place on the same hills and valleys where I was privileged to stand. I saw that the physical and geographical settings of the stories in my Bible were exactly as the Bible described.

I also interacted with the Jewish people—their faith and culture. They were the descendants, the relatives, of the ones I was reading about. Their faith was very much alive, and they were back in their ancient homeland just as God had promised their ancestors.

That's when the Bible stood up on its own two feet and came alive. It took on flesh and bones. I realized it was about real people and real places, that it was not only about spiritual stories for personal devotion or doctrinal study but filled with stories that were entirely true and accurate. My Bible went from two-dimensional to three-dimensional, full of color, meaning, accuracy, and life.

It had become 3D!

Jewish rabbis do more than just read the Bible; they study every line, word, and letter intensely. The Hebrew term for "study" is *lilmod*, which means "to search," "to seek," or "to examine intimately." And that's how we should read the Bible too—we should examine our Bibles and the words and stories within its pages thoroughly and intimately.

Yes, this type of reading takes more work! But God wants to know that you're interested in Him enough to dig a little deeper and take a bit more time in your study. In return He will meet you in the very pages of His Word.

With a little extra effort, you can advance from the inspirational and doctrinal levels of study to this life-changing 3D level. I am here to help. (And kudos for reading this book because it is a great place to begin!)

READING THE BIBLE IN CONTEXT

Not everyone can study in Israel, but we can all learn how to read the Bible in its original context. Here are four useful guidelines that will help you as you begin this journey to make your Bible 3D.

1. Consider the Historical Context

The Bible isn't just full of history; *it's a part of it*. God's Word informs us of what was happening within and around His people during major events and upheavals as kingdoms clashed and new ones emerged. That's why we must understand some ancient biblical history.

Knowing the correct historical context for a verse will help you understand what the author intended at the time of its writing. For example, a popular verse among many Christians is Jeremiah 29:11 (NIV): "'For I know the plans I have for you,' declares the LORD, 'plans to prosper you and not to harm you, plans to give you hope and a future.'" People often quote this, thinking it means nothing bad should ever happen in our lives because God has only good plans involving prosperity for us.

The historical context of this verse, however, exposes a different meaning. The Lord spoke it through the prophet Jeremiah at a time of exile. Judgment had fallen on Israel: God had removed His people from their land as punishment for their sins.

In Jeremiah 29:11, God is encouraging His people through Jeremiah that as they endure this terrible time of exile in Babylon, they should have hope because He has plans to restore them to their land. However, until that time arrives, they will endure exile and all its ramifications.

Another example of unspoken historical context comes from the New Testament regarding Herod the Great. Because Herod died soon after Jesus was born, he makes a relatively brief appearance in the Gospels, but his impact upon the world that Jesus was born into was astounding.

Jesus was born in Bethlehem, practically under the shadow of Herod's nearby palace called the Herodium. This antichrist-type maniac attempted to kill the child Jesus before He even reached two years of age. The gospel writers assume we know the larger context of who Herod was and his influence on the world in which Jesus was born. Despite being egotistical and paranoid, Herod was one of the top builders in the entire Roman Empire. He placed tiny Judea on the map with his man-made port at Caesarea and the magnificent temple complex in Jerusalem. His acclaim brought familiarity with the Jewish religion, which undoubtedly aided the eventual spread of the gospel from Judea throughout the Roman Empire.

2. Consider the Geographical Context

Most of the Bible takes place in what is now modern-day Israel. It's the stage God chose to place the characters of His grand narrative. God's placement of Israel on a particular piece of real estate was no accident—Israel was stationed in the middle of trade routes that brought other nations into contact with the Jewish people. It was a beautiful opportunity for Israel to influence godless people, reflect God's character, and draw them closer to Him:

> See, I have taught you statutes and rules ... that you should do them in the land that you are entering to take possession of it. Keep them and do them, for that will be your wisdom and your understanding *in the sight of the peoples*, who, when they hear all these statutes, will say, "Surely this great nation is a wise and understanding people." For what great nation is there that has a god so near to it as the LORD our God is to us, whenever we call upon him? (Deuteronomy 4:5–7 ESV, emphasis added)

Geography also played a crucial role in the life of Christ and helps explain some things not readily understood from the text. One example is the curious fact that the Gospel of Mark includes two stories about Jesus feeding large crowds (Mark 6:30–44; 8:1–10). Because each story varies slightly in its location and details, Bible critics claim they are but a variation of the same incident (and proof the text is corrupted). Both Mark and Matthew, however, quote Jesus pointing out the significance of the two events, particularly in the different numbers of baskets of food at each. For Jesus, the meaning of the numbers was so clear that He did not go on to explain what it was.

On the surface, the meaning of the mass feedings was that He provided food in abundance with more left over than the apostles started with. However, Northern Israel's geography offers a key to the deeper meaning of the miracle. At the time of Jesus, the western side of the Sea of Galilee was the Jewish side, and the eastern side was the gentile or pagan side known as the Decapolis.

Jesus fed crowds on both the Jewish and gentile sides to demonstrate that He is the bread of life for *all* people. The 12 baskets left over from the 5,000 on the Jewish side symbolized Jesus' provision for the 12 tribes of Israel (see Matthew 14:13–21; Mark 6:30–44; Luke 9:10–17; John 6:1–14). The 7 baskets left over from the 4,000 on the gentile side may have symbolized His mission to reach the nations (Jewish tradition upholds 70 as the number of nations). Both Jew and gentile would be part of the kingdom of God.

Understanding this difference in the two populations on opposite sides of the Sea of Galilee helps explain another odd story. It begins with Jesus calming the sea and then disembarking on the pagan side, where He encountered a demoniac (see Matthew 8:28–32; Mark 5:1–20). Jesus calls the demons out of the man and casts them into a herd of pigs, who then run into the water and die.

Jews did not raise pigs (they were considered unclean), so to start with this story makes no sense—unless you understand that Jesus was on the pagan side of the lake, where Ba'al worship was commonplace. Jesus had already demonstrated His power over Ba'al—the weather god—when He calmed the stormy sea. The description of the demoniac aligns with ancient Ba'al worship, which often happened in caves and involved self-mutilation and the sacrifice of pigs. When the herd of pigs plunged down the hillside into the sea and drowned, it destroyed the local Ba'al worship. Though never stated in the text, the entire story demonstrates Jesus' dominion over the power of Ba'al.

Geographical awareness also equips us to understand a final element in this story. Jesus told the former demoniac to stay on the gentile side of the lake and share the good news of the kingdom there (Mark 5:19–20). This instruction may seem odd for many Bible readers, considering Jesus had cautioned Peter and His other Jewish disciples against telling anyone He was Messiah. However, Jesus understood the danger of this information making its way to the authorities on the Jewish side of the lake; revealing who He was to the Jews had to wait for the right moment.

These geographical details not only make the events come alive but also attest to the accuracy of Scripture and affirm the benefit of becoming familiar with the land of the Bible.

3. Consider the Cultural Context

The cultural gap between ancient Israel and modern-day America is vast. If we're not careful, we may impose our own culture and worldview on the ancient text, which can lead to obvious interpretive issues. For example, much of the Bible is written from a Middle Eastern viewpoint, which emphasizes family and relationship over the individual. Because our western society values the individual over the group, we often miss meaningful details in the Scriptures.

Consider the story's beginning in Genesis, an eastern one that tells how God formed a family—a nation—to be His people who would carry out His plan to redeem humanity. After freeing His family from slavery in Egypt, God proposed to them a relationship—or covenant—likened to a marriage. If His people were loyal to Him, He would bestow upon them great blessings of relationship, protection, care, and provision. He would be their God (Genesis 17:8), and they would be His people (Leviticus 26:12).

In the New Testament we see God enlarging His family to include believers from every tribe and tongue who have been washed by the blood of Jesus. We are as wild olive branches that God has grafted into the family tree of faith that goes back to Abraham. While some natural branches were broken off due to unbelief, we are grafted in and receive sustenance from the great spiritual heritage of those who went before us. Now God has commissioned us with the great task of world missions, to gather what the Bible calls the "wheat" of God's harvest (see Matthew 9:36–38; cf. 13:30;

Revelation 14:14–16)—and then the book of Revelation says He will come and tabernacle with man (see Revelation 21:3).

God's plan from beginning to end was to create a family and dwell among them. But unfortunately, because so much of our western preaching focuses on salvation for the sake of the individual, we too often miss something critical: *the bigger picture of what God is doing.* By offering us this great salvation, He is adopting us into His family, a decidedly eastern concept to western eyes.

4. Consider the Audience

The Bible is a compilation of writings, each targeting a specific audience. Much of the Old Testament is written about and for the people of Israel. When we get to the New Testament, however, we find some writings have a Jewish audience in mind, while other portions are directed at a gentile audience. For example, out of the four Gospels, John wrote to a more Hellenized (Greek in culture) audience outside of Judea, which explains his unique approach and selective telling of the life of Christ.

John is the only Gospel that contains the story of Jesus turning the water into wine at a wedding. One explanation can be found in the popular belief throughout the Roman Empire in the god Dionysus, the founder of wine. Stories circulated throughout the empire of the miraculous growth of grapevines and the formation of wine in one day. Whenever these supposed miracles took place, people claimed Dionysus was present. John could have been establishing Jesus' predominance over Dionysus by retelling this story and concluding that the water-to-wine miracle "manifested His glory." In other words, *God* was present.

Other New Testament writings are letters written to various churches throughout the empire. To understand some of Paul's teachings regarding church practices, we must understand what was going on in *that* city and *that* church at the time. What pagan influences in society were affecting the early church through gentile converts? There are many examples—but I'll mention just one.

Paul's first letter to Timothy has some harsh passages that seem to prohibit women from teaching in the church. But a thorough reading of the book makes it clear that Timothy is dealing with the influences of the female cult of Diana headquartered in his city—Ephesus. People traveled from all over the empire to Ephesus to worship the goddess at the huge temple.

The cult of Diana involved many mystical theories, and it nurtured a twisted telling of the creation story in which Eve was the giver of knowledge to Adam and, therefore, men could only learn from women. The priestesses and prophetesses who conducted the cult of Diana also frequently delved into witchcraft. Paul was instructing Timothy to prevent these influences from infiltrating his church and prohibit women from teaching female domination of men. It is also important to note that Paul's words in the original Greek are challenging to translate, and other translations are possible that would make much more sense filtered through this cultic context.

5. Consider the Literary Context or Genre

Just as we must read a poem differently than a novel or science fiction differently than historical fiction, we must also consider the literary context or "genre" of the stories in the Bible.

The Bible includes several different genres:

- Narrative
- Law
- Poetry
- Wisdom
- Prophecy
- Gospel
- Letter
- History

Each genre has a purpose and reveals different things about God, the culture it was written in, and what was going on in the world of the Bible at that time. Therefore, if we expect to understand what the author intended to say, we should approach what we are reading according to its correct genre.

For example, we can ask questions about the text, such as: Is this verse in the middle of one of David's songs? If it is, remembering that we shouldn't always take song lyrics literally will help us more accurately unpack what we are reading. And approaching it for what it is—a song rather than, for example, history or law—will help us interpret it soundly.

We should interpret the Bible as it was originally written to be understood, which means we must consider its genre and context. God's Word is like a puzzle; to clearly understand its unity and the story behind the stories, we must put the puzzle pieces together. But we must do it responsibly, which requires filtering our reading through the correct lens. Doing so will help us better interpret God's Word and bring our Bibles to life.

TIPS AND TOOLS TO AID YOUR STUDY

A few tips and tools will help you in your Bible reading and studying journey.

Bible Translations

Understanding the difference between the many available Bible translations can be confusing, especially if you are buying your first Bible. However, it doesn't have to be! There are two primary types of translations:

1. **Word-for-word translation.** Word-for-word translations (also called "formal" translations) more literally reflect the Hebrew or Greek words in English. However, those translations tend to be slightly harder to understand because the translators have tried to be exact to another language. As a result, they can read a bit "bumpy" and seem disjointed.

2. **Thought-for-thought translation.** Thought-for-thought translations (also called "functional" or "dynamic equivalency" translations) take the meaning of a verse and express that in modern English. Thought-for-thought translations might be easier to read and understand, but they do not correspond word for word to the original.

The most well-known word-for-word translation—the gold standard for this kind of translation—is the King James Version (KJV). The difficulty with the King James Version is that it was written in English of about 400 years ago, so many of the words don't make sense—they sound formal, obsolete, or archaic. For example, most modern readers won't know what "appertain" means in Jeremiah 10:6–7: "For to thee doth it *appertain*: forasmuch as among all the wise men of the nations and in all their kingdoms, there is none like unto thee."

The New King James Version (NKJV) is also considered a word-for-word translation but is a bit easier to read. This is because translators took the King James Version and edited it to be more modern in its English usage while retaining some of its formality and structure. A newer word-for-word translation growing in popularity is the English Standard Version (ESV).

A middle-of-the-road translation is the New International Version (NIV), one of the best-selling Bibles. It's a combination of a word-for-word and thought-for-thought translation, making it easy to read and understand.

Many other translations are well-respected, and you can't go wrong with most of them—but the New King James Version (NKJV), the New International Version (NIV), and the English Standard Version (ESV) are among the best sellers. You may consider using multiple translations while you study, which will give you a well-rounded understanding of the verse or passage at hand. Doing so demonstrates good scholarship and will also help you see what the author was communicating in new ways.

Study Bibles

In addition to choosing a Bible based on the translation, you also may want to consider a study Bible. Most basic Bibles have a few maps and a topical index in the back, but study Bibles include much more! A study Bible can be two or three times thicker than a regular Bible because the publisher has added commentary, articles, word studies, and study aids. Some study Bibles focus on a theme, like archaeology or cultural backgrounds. For example, articles in the *Life Application Bible* concentrate on applying the Bible to daily life. The *Holy Land Study Bible* takes readers on a visual tour of biblical times. The *New Inductive Study Bible* guides you through the inductive study approach. And the *Apologetics Study Bible* helps people understand, defend, and proclaim their beliefs in an age of increasing moral and spiritual relativism.

Another excellent study Bible that I use and love is *The Complete Jewish Study Bible*. Its detailed notes and comprehensive study material help Jewish and Christian readers understand and connect with the essence of their faith—God's redemptive plan for His people. It's packed with over 100 articles on topics like Jewish customs, messianic prophecy, the names of God, Shabbat, the Torah, and more. Plus, it follows the Jewish order of the Tanakh's (Old Testament) books, offers the original Hebrew names for all people, places, and concepts, and includes quotes and excerpts from well-known rabbis and scholars.

Cross-References

Most basic Bibles will also have "cross-references." For example, many verses will have a footnote listing another verse or verses in the Bible about the same subject or additional verses that use the same word. To learn more about a topic or word in a particular verse, you can follow the cross-reference and see where else the Bible uses it.

Bible Apps

Some students of the Bible may also choose to use a Bible app. They're typically free and allow you to read the Bible anywhere once installed on your phone. Plus, you can do word searches or find verses quickly while on the go and use your phone to set reminders for scheduled reading. Some Bible apps even have prepared Bible reading plans, commentaries, and concordances.

Chronological Bibles

The Bible is organized *somewhat* chronologically; it begins with creation and ends with the future return of Jesus, and the Old Testament covers the period of history that precedes that of the New Testament. However, when reading the Bible from cover to cover, it can be hard to follow the story; the order of the books within these sections is not necessarily chronological, and multiple books can cover the same event. For example, you can read the historical account of an event in one book and prophetic writings about that event in others.

Portions of the Bible are also a bit tedious to read through. Most people start reading through the Bible in Genesis—a book full of fascinating stories and bigger-than-life characters. The second book, Exodus, is also easy to read. But many people drop out in the third book, Leviticus, with its lists of laws, regulations, and sacrifices. And reading through the New Testament can become laborious because it begins with four Gospels, each retelling a slightly different version of the same stories.

Therefore, if you want to read the Bible from beginning to end, I recommend using a true chronological Bible. Chronological Bibles have rearranged portions of the Bible so that the events and writings show in the order they happened.

Though there are many excellent chronological Bibles, I recommend *The Daily Bible*. It is unique, and I believe it is the easiest to use. The editor, Mr. F. LaGard Smith, not only rearranged the verses chronologically but divided them into 365 daily readings and provided an introductory summary to most of them. He also combined repetitive passages into one narrative. Plus, every verse is footnoted in the margin, so you know where the author pulled each one. It's the Word of God magnificently compiled as a single narrative.

By committing to just 20 minutes a day, in just 365 days, you can read the entire *Daily Bible*. Even beginners can start to comprehend the overarching story of the Bible thanks to F. LaGard Smith's labor of love.

My "Walk Thru the Bible" Course

To assist you on this journey, I have recorded weekly teachings based on *The Daily Bible* reading schedule called "Walk Thru the Bible." This way you can read through the Bible with me, and I can help you stay focused on the story behind the stories and share little details from my years of travel in Israel. I will help you as you make your way through *The Daily Bible* from Genesis to Revelation. (See Appendix B: Recommended Resources at the end of this book for the link to sign up for my "Walk Thru the Bible" course.)

Another Handy Resource

Another helpful tool I recommend is an eight-colored mechanical pencil made by Pentel. I use it to highlight verses as I'm reading. My Bible is full of highlights, and the eight colors help me track by subject. For example, every blue highlight indicates something about Israel and the Jewish people that I want to remember. Yellow is related to the Holy Spirit specifically or a spiritual principle in general. I use red to mark historical facts or important numbers and pink for salvation and Jesus. Green is for those moments when Scripture jumps off the page and into my heart—when the Holy Spirit uses a particular verse or passage to affirm, encourage, or give me direction for the day. You can create a color program that works best for you.

No matter which translation you choose or whether you supplement your study with a study or chronological Bible or not, what's most important is *starting*. Ask God to "make wise the simple" and "enlighten your eyes" (Psalm 19:7–8) as you begin the journey—He will be faithful to bring your Bible to life when you commit to reading it with Him.

CHAPTER THREE

The Story of the Bible

Even if you have been banished to the most distant land under the heavens, from there the LORD your God will gather you and bring you back.
—Deuteronomy 30:4 NIV

I am one of those people who cannot see the forest for the trees. I am detail-oriented and tend to focus on *my* tree in *my little corner* of the forest. Over the years I have had to train myself to step back and look at the forest because it does not come naturally to me. But it is so rewarding when I do. Only then do I see how my tree relates to all the other trees in the forest, which helps me understand how to tend my tree *better*.

I have also found that this practice aids my comprehension of the Bible. Because the Bible is packed with so many stories, it's easy to become lost in the weeds and forget the broader narrative. And yet understanding the overarching story of the Bible is paramount to understanding how each story relates to the others.

In this chapter, I want to help you do just this—understand God's perfect, beautiful, grand story of redemption. But first, let's deal with a serious misperception, a common misunderstanding that results from oversimplifying the biblical narrative.

DID GOD MAKE A MISTAKE?

Often people approach the Bible as if it is made up of two parts: the old part and the new. And the assumption is that the new is not only better but that it has replaced the old.

The problem with this approach is twofold. First, it sounds like God had an old plan that failed, so He came up with a new plan with a new people, sort of like a Plan A and a Plan B. *But what kind of God has a plan that fails?*

Another problem with this approach is that some Christians dismiss the Old Testament and only read the New. As a result, they rob themselves of understanding the overarching story of the Bible. They risk misunderstanding God's character and dealings with man and won't grasp God's profound faithfulness to fulfill His Word and His promises. When we do not teach the Old Testament, Jesus can come across as a mythological Greek god appearing out of nowhere instead of arriving in a context that had been prepared since before God laid the foundations of the earth.

GOD'S PLAN TO REDEEM HUMANITY

The Bible tells the story of God's plan to redeem fallen humankind. And Paul said in Ephesians that this plan is eternal:

> For he chose us in him *before* the creation of the world to be holy and blameless in his sight. In love he predestined us for adoption to *sonship through Jesus Christ*. (Ephesians 1:4–5 NIV, emphasis added)

God's eternal plan was to adopt us into His family through Jesus Christ. This means that Jesus' atoning death on the cross was always Plan A, even before He created the world or chose Abraham to birth a nation. John affirmed this in Revelation 13:8 when he wrote that Jesus is "the Lamb slain from the foundation of the world."

God was not surprised when the Jewish leaders rejected Jesus' messianic credentials and handed Him over to be crucified. In fact, God used their disbelief. He fully understands how frail man is, so His plan depends solely on Him. Yet He uses man to carry out His plan.

Knowing that the Bible tells one story—with no disconnect—we can now begin to unpack what that story is.

THE BIBLE BEGINS WITH CREATION

Genesis 1–11 begins with creation and ends with humankind in utter despair. God creates Adam and Eve to live in a beautiful garden in fellowship with Him, but they rebel and eat from the forbidden tree. Their sin gets them banished from the garden, and from this point through Genesis 11, the Bible reveals the sad story of humanity's decline. Sin eventually becomes so rampant that God sends a flood over the entire earth, and only eight people are saved: Noah, his wife, their three sons, and their wives. These eight people then repopulate the planet.

But sadly, despite God's promise to Noah—that He would never judge the earth by flood again—man continues to sin. People fall into idolatry. They are destined to be separated from God forever and have no hope.

THE WATERSHED MOMENT OF THE BIBLE

But then, in Genesis 12, God spoke to a man named Abraham, and everything changed:

> Get out of your country, from your family and from your father's house, *to a land that I will show you. I will make you a great nation*; I will bless you and make your name great; and you shall be a blessing. I will bless those who bless you, and I will curse him who curses

you; *and in you all the families of the earth shall be blessed.* (1–3, emphasis added)

Genesis 12:1–3 is the watershed moment of the Bible. Abraham was a gentile living in Ur of the Chaldees (ancient Mesopotamia). Tradition has it that his family members were idol-makers. But in these first verses of Genesis 12, the God of the universe announces something amazing to this man: His plan to redeem the world. Paul said the phrase "all the families of the earth will be blessed" in Genesis 12:3 was the first time the gospel was preached because it referred to Christ (see Galatians 3:7–9).

God told Abraham to follow Him to a land that He would show him and that He would make him into a great nation. Then God said He would bless Abraham and any person or nation that blesses him and his descendants—the Jewish people. Ultimately, God will bless *all* the families of the earth with this amazing plan of redemption.

However, God had called Abraham to do something impossible: father a nation. Abraham could not bring forth descendants because Sarah, his wife, was barren. Interestingly, God also charged the nation He would create out of Abraham with an equally impossible task—to be the vehicle of His redemptive plan.

THE CALLING OF ISRAEL

Abraham's descendants, through Isaac and then Jacob (God later changed Jacob's name to Israel), would become known as the children of Israel and later as the Jewish people. However, their calling remained the same: to be the vehicle of God's eternal plan of redemption. Through the children of Israel, God would reveal His character; the need for holiness and righteousness so that all people could walk in fellowship with Him; and how to be forgiven for failures and sins through the death of the Lamb slain for our transgressions.

They were to bring this plan out of eternity and into real time and space. You could say that they were a "birthing" people.

A Birthing Call

Just as God called Abraham to "birth" a nation (Israel), God also called that nation to "birth" His plan of redemption into all the earth. The descendants of Abraham were to be the carriers—or the vehicle—of God's plan to restore all things.

The apostle Paul discussed the incredible redemptive gifts God gave the Jewish people that would, in turn, be passed to gentiles:

> Theirs is the adoption to sonship; theirs the divine glory, the covenants, the receiving of the law, the temple worship and the promises. Theirs are the patriarchs, and from them is traced the human ancestry of the Messiah, who is God over all, forever praised! (Romans 9:4–5 NIV)

According to Paul, God did all these things through Israel, and we are the beneficiaries. All of God's promises in Genesis 12 are theirs.

In Romans 3:2 Paul referred to Israel as the custodians of these promises, saying the Jewish people "have been entrusted with the very words of God" (NIV). They have guarded Scripture, cared for it, and carried it through history. We have the Bible today because of the Jewish people's care and custodianship of it.

Most importantly, we are saved by the Jewish Messiah. Jesus said in John 4:22 that "Salvation is of the Jews" because it would be the Jewish Messiah—sent to the house of Israel—who would die on the cross. And though gentile believers benefit from His death and resurrection, salvation is first and foremost to the Jews (Romans 1:16; 2:10; cf. Luke 24:47).

The Promise of Land

God had not only promised descendants with a mission in Genesis 12 but also land. A few chapters later He revealed that land was Canaan. The land of Canaan would be an everlasting possession for Abraham's descendants because it was part of an eternal covenant:

> I will establish my covenant as an *everlasting covenant* between me and you and your descendants after you for the generations to come, to be your God and the God of your descendants after you. The whole land of Canaan, where you now reside as a foreigner, I will give as an *everlasting possession* to you and your descendants after you; and I will be their God. (Genesis 17:7–8 NIV, emphasis added)

The land is key to the covenant God made with Abraham. The land was to be like a stage, an entry point, from where He would do His most extraordinary works. It was their inheritance as His children and from where He would carry out His great plan of redemption.

There was just one catch. Because the land belonged to the Lord, and as such was a holy land, God required that His children live holy and righteous lives and be obedient to live on the land He was giving them. It would always be their possession, but their right of domicile on it was conditional.

God wanted His people to live righteously to reflect Him and His character to a watching world. Israel's holiness was such a serious matter that He warned the Jewish people if they were not obedient, they would be uprooted from the land and "scattered":

> If you do not carefully follow all the words of this law, which are written in this book, and do not revere this glorious and awesome name—the LORD your God … Just as it pleased the LORD to make you prosper and increase in number, so it will please him to ruin and destroy you. *You will be uprooted from the land* you are entering to possess. Then the LORD will *scatter you among all*

nations, from one end of the earth to the other. (Deuteronomy 28:58, 63–64 NIV, emphasis added)

Promise of Return

Even if they were scattered throughout the earth, however, God also promised to one day return them to their land:

> Even if you have been banished to the most distant land under the heavens, from there the LORD your God will gather you and bring you back. He will bring you to the land that belonged to your ancestors, and you will take possession of it. He will make you more prosperous and numerous than your ancestors. The LORD your God will circumcise your hearts and the hearts of your descendants, so that you may love him with all your heart and with all your soul, and live. (Deuteronomy 30:4–6 NIV)

GOD CONFIRMS HIS PROMISES TO ABRAHAM

God not only made promises to Abraham, but He made a covenant with him to confirm them. We read about this covenant in Genesis 15:

> "Bring Me a three-year-old heifer, a three-year-old female goat, a three-year-old ram, a turtledove, and a young pigeon." Then [Abraham] brought all these to Him and cut them in two, down the middle, and placed each piece opposite the other; but he did not cut the birds in two. (vv. 9–10)[1]

Notice that God told Abraham to gather specific animals as required for the ceremony—and that Abraham knew what to do with them.

---

[1] Adam Clarke notes that every animal God allows or commands to be sacrificed under Mosaic law is included in this list. Clarke, Adam, "Commentary on Genesis 15:9," *The Adam Clarke Commentary*, 8 vols. (Krill Press), 2015.

Though this practice might seem strange to modern Bible readers, covenant-making rituals were common among different cultures and societies in ancient biblical times.[2]

After Abraham displayed the carcasses, Genesis 15:11 says vicious vultures attacked the bodies. Abraham fought off the savage birds until dusk, and then he fell into a deep sleep. While sleeping, Abraham saw a smoking oven and burning torch passing between the pieces. Genesis 15:18 says, "On that same day, the LORD *made* a covenant with Abram [Abraham], saying, 'To your descendants I have given this land'" (emphasis added).

The word "made" in the original Hebrew is *kārat*, which means "to cut," in the sense of making an alliance demonstrated through the actual cutting of flesh. The word "covenant" is *berit*, which means "a pact" or "an alliance of friendship." Therefore, the phrase "made a covenant" literally means "to cut a pact." Passing between the carcasses was a symbolic act that communicated the consequences for the one who broke the alliance.

Interestingly, in this case, God—represented by the "smoking oven and burning torch"—was the only one who passed between the cut-up animals while Abraham slept. This means that *keeping* the terms of this covenant is entirely dependent upon God and not on anything Abraham or his descendants did or didn't do.

Admittedly, the "smoking oven and burning torch" that passed between the animal pieces is peculiar imagery. However, Scripture gives clues to what—or who—this smoking oven and burning torch might be. Repeatedly in Scripture, God's presence is associated with smoke and fire, such as in the wilderness when "the LORD went before them by day in a pillar of cloud to lead the way, and by night in a pillar of fire to give them light" (Exodus 13:21).

Thus, in Genesis 15, it was God "passing between the pieces,"

---

[2] David Noel Friedman, ed., *The Anchor Bible Dictionary* (New York: Doubleday, 1992), s.v. "covenant."

confirming His promises and taking on responsibility for their fulfillment. The covenant God made affirmed to Abraham, "You have my word." It was not up to Abraham to fulfill it—God Himself would cause these promises to come to pass.

SUFFERING DUE TO THE COVENANT

However, that is not all that happened while Abraham slept. Verse 12 says that a deep horror filled his soul. It was as if Abraham knew that just as the vultures had almost destroyed the covenant by consuming the carcasses, evil "vultures" would always be after this covenant God had made with him. Abraham's people would suffer great opposition due to this special agreement and calling upon them.

Immediately afterward God revealed to Abraham that before his descendants inherited the land, they would go into slavery in a foreign land:

> Know for certain that for four hundred years your descendants will be strangers in a country not their own and that they will be enslaved and mistreated there. (Genesis 15:13 NIV)

Sure enough, Abraham's descendants went to Egypt to escape a famine, where they were eventually enslaved.

MOSAIC COVENANT WITH THE CHILDREN OF ISRAEL

After being released from Egyptian slavery and miraculously crossing the Red (or Reed) Sea, the children of Israel were introduced to the God who had set them free. Through Moses He revealed His name and His will and proposed a relationship: if they walked in obedience to Him and pursued righteousness, they would be His people, and He would be their God. The people agreed and then built a tabernacle for God's presence to dwell in their midst.

It was now time for them to receive their allotted inheritance promised to Abraham—the land of Canaan. But the people followed the negative reports of 10 of the 12 spies and lacked the faith to take the land. As a result, they wandered for 40 years in the desert until a new generation matured and was ready to take possession of the land. The books of Exodus, Leviticus, Numbers, Deuteronomy, and Joshua unpack this pivotal story in Israel's history.

TAKING POSSESSION OF THE PROMISED LAND

Once they entered Canaan, each of the 12 tribes was given an allotment of land. Initially, Israel was a tribal federacy with judges who ruled over the various tribes. God established these judges to represent Him as King on Earth to the people (see Exodus 18:15–16). But the people observed that the gentile nations they lived among had human kings and centralized governments. So they asked the prophet Samuel for a king to be like the other nations:

> Then all the elders of Israel gathered together and came to Samuel at Ramah, and said to him, "Look, you are old, and your sons do not walk in your ways. *Now make us a king to judge us like all the nations.*" (1 Samuel 8:4–5, emphasis added)

Fear and earthly mindedness had caused the people to cry out, "We want a king! All the nations around us have a king!" They had reached a point where they did not trust God or that He would protect and provide for them. In response to the people's demand, God gave them what they wanted in 1 Samuel 8:7:

> The LORD said to Samuel, "Heed the voice of the people in all that they say to you; for they have not rejected you, but they have rejected Me, that I should not reign over them."

Note that the people were not rejecting Samuel as their leader—they were rejecting God, and this rejection would have dire consequences. (You can read the stories about Israel's first king, Saul, followed by King David, in three historical books: 1 and 2 Samuel and 1 Chronicles.)

DAVIDIC KINGDOM: THE HIGHLIGHT OF ISRAEL'S HISTORY

King David's reign is considered the highlight of Israel's history, for David had a heart after the Lord (1 Samuel 13:14). During David's reign, Israel's kingdom was united, prosperous, and large. King David brought the tabernacle and the ark of the covenant up to Jerusalem and worshiped before the Lord with all his might. He wanted to build a temple to the Lord but was told not to. Instead, God was going to do something profound for David.

THE DAVIDIC COVENANT

In 2 Samuel 7:16, God made a promise to David that would impact the entire world:

> And your house and your kingdom shall be established forever before you. Your throne shall be established forever.

In this verse, God promised King David a throne—but interestingly, God said that throne would extend beyond David's lifetime. It would be an eternal throne. This promise is also known as the Davidic covenant, and like the Abrahamic covenant, God didn't require David to do anything. Both covenants are "unconditional covenants" because God will cause what He promised to come to pass regardless of whether people obey.

David's Throne in Jerusalem

David established Jerusalem as the capital of his kingdom, but 2 Chronicles 6:6 indicates it was ultimately God's choice:

Yet *I have chosen* Jerusalem, that My name may be there, and I have chosen David to be over My people Israel. (Emphasis added)

Out of the whole earth, God chose Jerusalem as the place for His name and from where David would rule over God's people. David's son, Solomon, became king after his father and built the First Temple in Jerusalem—a magnificent architectural building for the day.

Sin Brings Division to the Kingdom

However, Solomon allowed sin to creep in; despite being known as the wisest man in the nation, he worshiped idols, a terrible sin in God's eyes.

Eventually, when Solomon's son, Rehoboam, took the throne, the kingdom of Israel split into two parts. The kingdom in the north would be called Israel, and the kingdom in the south—which included Jerusalem—would become known as Judah.

Division is always a sign of sin, evidenced in Northern Israel's continued decline. Sadly, Israel's leaders even erected alternate, idolatrous worship sites to stop their people from worshiping in the temple in Jerusalem.

THE FIRST EXILE

Prophets like Hosea, Amos, and Isaiah began to warn Israel that judgment would come if she did not return to the Lord. They knew of coming judgment before it happened because in Israel's law, God had already told His people judgment would result *when* the nation fell into sin—and judgment would be the exile of the Jewish people from the land (Deuteronomy 4:25–30).

The prophets saw the writing on the wall. They witnessed Israel's decline and began to warn the kingdom of Israel, calling the people to repentance. But sadly, Israel didn't listen, and in 722 BC, God used the Assyrian Empire to enact His judgment. Their army invaded, took over the kingdom of the north, and exiled the people of Israel to Assyria.

The kingdoms of Israel and Judah in the ninth century BC (source: commons.wikimedia.org)

In like manner, the Southern Kingdom of Judah continued in idolatry and outright rebellion against God. And soon prophets like Isaiah and Jeremiah began issuing similar warnings to Judah: return to the Lord, or judgment will come. This time, judgment came in the form of the Babylonian army under King Nebuchadnezzar, who had conquered the Assyrian Empire. From 607 to 586 BC, Jews were taken into captivity in Babylon several times until the final siege against Jerusalem in 586 BC.

The first exile had occurred in two stages over a period of 150 years but was now complete. The temple was destroyed, and no government remained in the land.

THE FIRST RETURN

God's people were devastated, as shown in Psalm 137, a lament of longing for the Jewish community stripped from their home, Jerusalem. The psalmist described Israel by the rivers of Babylon weeping "when we remembered Zion" (v. 1). God told the exiles through Jeremiah to settle in, build houses and dwell in them, plant gardens and eat their fruit, and marry and have sons and daughters (Jeremiah 29:5–6).

However, their banishment from Israel would not be permanent—Jeremiah also prophesied their exile to Babylon would last 70 years:

> And this whole land shall be a desolation and an astonishment, and these nations shall serve the king of Babylon seventy years. (Jeremiah 25:11; cf. 2 Chronicles 36:17–21)

King Nebuchadnezzar identified men from Israel's royal household who were handsome with an aptitude for learning to be trained in Babylonian ways and put into the king's service (Daniel 1:1–6). One of these men was the prophet Daniel. Nebuchadnezzar also chose three of Daniel's fellow citizens from Judea and gave them new names to disassociate them from their Hebrew roots and assimilate them into Babylonian culture.

Near the end of Judah's 70-year exile, Daniel read Jeremiah's prophecy, realized the exile was nearing its end, and began to pray for the people's return. Soon after Daniel prayed, the Persian Empire, under King Cyrus, took over the Babylonian Empire and released all the subjects of the kingdom to return to their homelands and rebuild their temples.

The Jewish exiles were allowed to return to rebuild the city of Jerusalem and the temple (see the books of Ezra and Nehemiah). This return from the first exile initiated a great revival back in the land and was the beginning of the Second Temple period, which lasted almost 600 years.

THE STAGE IS SET FOR REDEMPTION

The people's return to the land and the rebuilding of Jerusalem prepared the stage for the birth, life, and ministry of Jesus and His death on the cross. Profoundly, the prophet Isaiah had foreseen the return of the Jews to their land as well as coming restoration—the suffering Messiah who would atone for the sins of His people (Isaiah 53). True to His word, God had already declared in the Hebrew Scriptures "what is still to come" (Isaiah 46:10 NIV).

Jesus fulfilled many prophecies and arrived at just the right time. He suffered on the cross for the sins of the world—our redemption was won!

THE CHURCH IS BORN

After Jesus was crucified, He was placed in a tomb, and on the third day, was raised from the dead. He appeared on Earth for 40 days. Right before Jesus ascended to heaven, He instructed His disciples to go back to Jerusalem and "wait for the Promise of the Father" (Acts 1:4), the Holy Spirit. Jesus had to return to the throne of heaven to send the Holy Spirit.

Once He did, the church was born. The book of Acts and corresponding letters of the apostles to various churches recount how the apostles began to take the gospel throughout the Roman Empire: from Judea and Samaria to the uttermost parts of the world.

THE SECOND EXILE

The brutal Roman Empire, however, still ruled the ancient land of Canaan—now called Judea—and the headquarters of the Jewish faith. In AD 67, the Roman forces began a siege of Jerusalem, and by AD 70, Rome had taken over the city, destroying it and the temple. The first-century Jewish historian Josephus described the destruction of Jerusalem, writing that "no other city has ever endured such horrors, and no generation in history has fathered such wickedness":[3]

> As the flames shot into the air the Jews sent up a cry that matched the calamity and dashed to the rescue, with no thought now of saving their lives or husbanding their strength; for that which hitherto they had guarded so devotedly was disappearing before their eyes.[4]

Many of the people of Israel were either killed or fled for their lives, which became known as the second exile. Jesus warned of this exile in Luke 21:5–38 when He prophesied the temple's destruction, saying, "Not one stone shall be left upon another that shall not be thrown down" (v. 6). Note Jesus' specific instructions to the Jews in verse 21 concerning what they were to do when this happened:

> Let those who are in Judea flee to the mountains, let those in the city get out, and let those in the country not enter the city. (NIV)

Jesus warned His disciples that when they saw the temple destroyed to "run into the hills." Indeed, this is what happened. When Rome was sacking Jerusalem, the Jewish believers in Jesus remembered His words and escaped into the surrounding hills; few perished in the fall of

---

[3] Flavius Josephus, *The Jewish War*, 292, 323.
[4] Josephus, *Jewish War*, 292, 323.

Jerusalem. But unfortunately, when they returned, they were seen as traitors by the Jewish leaders who had stayed and suffered the siege and fall of the city.

Soon after Jerusalem's destruction, John, now elderly, wrote what would become the last book of the Bible: Revelation. John had been banished to the isle of Patmos, where he had an awe-inspiring encounter with the risen Christ that weakened him to the point that he fell to the ground "as though dead" (Revelation 1:17 NIV). John also had subsequent visions of the future—including a vision of the return of Jesus, which brings the New Testament canon to a close.

But the story of the Bible continues even today. We know this because the Bible foretold future events that have not happened yet. And until those events occur, the story that began in Genesis is not over.

THE STORY OF THE BIBLE CONTINUES TODAY

Many biblical prophecies are being fulfilled in our day concerning the return of the Jewish people to their homeland. This brings great excitement and anticipation for those prophecies not yet fulfilled.

A Second Return to the Land of Israel

Isaiah 11:11 affirms that one day, God will raise His hand *a second time* and regather the outcasts of Israel:

> It shall come to pass in that day that the Lord shall set His hand again *the second time* to recover the remnant of His people who are left. (Emphasis added)

We'll unpack more about this idea of a second exile and return in chapter 6. But for now, be encouraged to handle the word of truth diligently and correctly (2 Timothy 2:15). In the case of Israel's regathering, it's clear there is more than one.

The return from Babylon was the first return from exile. But today we see Jewish exiles returning *a second time*—just as Isaiah prophesied. This time, however, instead of returning from one nation, Jews are being gathered from the many nations to which they have been scattered.

While a remnant of Jews had remained in the land during the previous exiles, significant waves of immigration began to expand their numbers and plant new communities. Since the late 1800s, Jews have been returning to the land from over 150 nations—a miracle in our day, to be sure—including Russia, Ukraine, Ethiopia, India, the United States, and Canada.

As of September 2022, Israel's population included just over 7 million Jews. To date, more than 3.3 million immigrants have made Aliyah to Israel since the state's establishment.[5] They are coming from the north, south, east, and west—just as the Bible promises:

> He will set up a banner for the nations, and will assemble the outcasts of Israel, and gather together the dispersed of Judah from the four corners of the earth. (Isaiah 11:12)

Jerusalem under Jewish Sovereignty

Before Jesus was crucified, He told His disciples that "Jerusalem will be trampled by Gentiles until the times of the Gentiles are fulfilled" (Luke 21:24), a prophecy foretelling the return of Jerusalem to Jewish sovereignty.

For almost 2,000 years, Jerusalem was under gentile control. However, since the 1967 Six Day War, Jerusalem has been under Israeli (Jewish) control.

Future Restoration of the Kingdom to Israel

Another interesting statement Jesus made indicated a future restoration of

---

[5] Times of Israel Staff, "Israel's Jewish population passes 7 million on the eve of Rosh Hashanah," *The Times of Israel*, September 25, 2022.

Israel not just as a modern state but as a kingdom under the Lordship of their God. Right before He ascended to heaven, the disciples asked Jesus, "Lord, will You at this time restore the kingdom to Israel?" (Acts 1:6). Jesus didn't disagree or respond by saying, "You're wrong." Instead, He answered their question, saying, "It is not for you to know times or seasons which the Father has put in His own authority" (Acts 1:7). Though it's exciting to watch these prophecies come to pass before our eyes, Jesus was clear that the exact timing of the restoration of Israel was not for them—and therefore not for us—to know.

Nonetheless, the Jewish people are returning to their homeland in our day, the same land God promised them through Abraham centuries ago. And Jerusalem is back under Jewish sovereignty.

God is once again setting the stage.

THE RETURN OF THE KING

We are privileged to be living in this hour! The story of God's love for a fallen world is the story of His choice of a people through whom He gave us the amazing redemptive gifts of the law, the promises, the temple, and the Messiah. They also gave us the Bible—not just the Old Testament but also the New.

Through faith in Jesus, gentiles can tap into this rich heritage and become a part of it. In Romans 11:24 the apostle Paul said gentiles are like wild olive branches grafted by faith into a natural olive tree of the faithful that goes all the way back to Abraham. Through Christ Jesus we become a part of that "tree," and we can grow and be sustained by the sustenance of its roots.

We are spiritually indebted to the Jewish people because they have fulfilled God's call to bring His plan of world redemption to the earth, even though that plan has not yet been completely fulfilled.

Jesus paid the price on the cross and said, "It is finished" (John 19:30). But even though we have redemption through His blood (Ephesians 1:7), the story is not over until Jesus returns to the earth. Only then will all of God's promises in the Old Testament be fulfilled. And that day is coming! Consider Jesus' final words in Revelation 22:

> Behold, I am coming quickly. ... I am the Alpha and the Omega, the Beginning and the End, the First and the Last. ... I am the *Root and the Offspring of David*, the Bright and Morning Star. (vv. 12–13, 16, emphasis added)

Jesus will return to sit on the throne of the eternal kingdom God promised David over 3,000 years ago, which means God's promises to Abraham and David are valid today. His covenants with them are still in place. Moreover, the calling on the Jewish people to mediate those covenants has not changed—the apostle Paul said the Jews are beloved by God due to their calling, which can never be revoked (Romans 11:26–29).

It's only when we understand this amazing story that the Bible becomes the most exciting book on the planet!

It becomes 3D.

CHAPTER FOUR

How Should Christians Read the Old Testament?

And beginning at Moses and all the Prophets, He expounded to them in all the Scriptures the things concerning Himself.
—Luke 24:27

Admittedly, the Old Testament can be difficult to understand—at least harder than the New Testament. It contains concepts and cultural differences that don't make sense to our twenty-first-century minds and may even be confusing. As a result, some people ignore the Old Testament, even declare it irrelevant, and say we should spend our time focused "only on Jesus." What they mean is to only study the New Testament.

The first verse of the first book of the New Testament, however, begins with Jesus' genealogy: He is the son of David, the son of Abraham. But who is David? And who is Abraham? There's no way for New Testament believers to understand who Jesus is and what He came to do without an understanding of the Old Testament.

I want to help you learn how to read and defend the Old Testament instead of ignoring it. Without it, we rob Christianity of its foundation, and we will never understand who Jesus was, what He came to do, and why He must come again! Perhaps you are still a little skeptical about the importance of the Old Testament, so let me share a few thoughts.

THE OLD TESTAMENT IS NOT OLD—IT IS OLDER

The Bible has two parts: the Old Testament and the New Testament. Our early church fathers[6] gave the two parts those names, decided which books to include and the order in which they would appear, and placed the Old Testament in front of the New Testament.

Unfortunately, when people think of the Old Testament, they sometimes stumble over the word "old." The New Testament sounds more exciting—it's "new," so they immediately think it's more pertinent to them and that perhaps they don't have to deal with the Old.

If only our church fathers had chosen to call them the Hebrew Scriptures (almost all the books of the Old Testament are originally in Hebrew) as opposed to the Greek Scriptures (New Testament manuscripts are in Greek). Alas, they did not, and we are left fighting the idea that one part of our Bible is old and, therefore, less important.

Admittedly, the Old Testament includes some difficult sections and concepts; skeptics often use these challenging sections as a tool to bash the Christian faith altogether. Many a college student has heard people accusing the Bible of error and being full of archaic ideas. If they did not know how to defend the Old Testament or explain those troublesome verses, they may have struggled with their faith—or lost their faith entirely.

To make the Christian faith more appealing to skeptics, some Christians have disregarded the Old Testament altogether. However, we mustn't put the Old Testament aside but instead learn how to properly approach the whole counsel of God, which includes the Old Testament.

---

[6] The early church fathers, though not perfect, were concerned about (1) ensuring the gospel was proclaimed as the apostles intended and (2) rooting out and exposing false doctrine. They helped formulate the theology most Christians would agree with today.

THE OLD TESTAMENT HAS NOT BEEN REPLACED
The idea that the Old Testament is irrelevant is usually just another way of saying the New Testament has replaced it. But this idea is inaccurate and based on erroneous theology known as "Replacement Theology."

In short, Replacement Theology teaches that the old covenant has been replaced with the new covenant. Therefore, the Jews have been replaced by the Christian church as God's chosen people. Unfortunately, this teaching creates a disconnect between the Old and New Testaments—the first becomes something like a Plan A that failed, and the second, a new Plan B. Because this approach to Scripture is so prevalent among Christians, let's unpack it more.

THE OLD TESTAMENT IS NOT THE OLD COVENANT
The church fathers chose to put a piece of paper in the front of the first section of the Bible, calling it the "Old Testament." The word "testament" is the same as the word "covenant," which means "Old Testament" can be translated as "old covenant." But that doesn't mean that the Old Testament is a covenant.

The Old Testament is a book made up of 39 different books written by about 30 authors. It tells a narrative that covers nearly 2,500 years of history. It talks about several different covenants, of which four are considered major: the Abrahamic, Mosaic, Davidic, and new covenants:

- The *Abrahamic covenant* promised the birth of a lineage of people whom God would charge with blessing the world.
- The *Mosaic covenant* was likened to a marriage between God and the nation of Israel.
- The *Davidic covenant* promised an everlasting throne to the lineage of David.

- The *new covenant* promised forgiveness of sins and the writing of the law upon the hearts of God's people, thereby sealing their relationship with Him forever.

Descriptions of the first three covenants are sprinkled throughout the Old Testament, but Jeremiah 31 is the primary description of the new covenant. In verse 31 God announces a coming day when He will initiate this new covenant with His people:

> Behold, the days are coming, says the LORD, when I will make a *new covenant* with the house of Israel and with the house of Judah. (Emphasis added; see also vv. 32–34)

Notice that God makes this covenant with the houses of Israel and Judah. What about the gentiles? Do they partake in it? And if they do, how?

Gentiles are grafted into this covenant through faith in Jesus, who literally "cut" the new covenant by dying on the cross. By God's incredible grace, gentiles "who once were far off" but "have been brought near by the blood of Christ" (Ephesians 2:13) can now fully participate in all God's promises given to Israel.

The point is this: we cannot equate the Old Testament with some concept of "old covenant," just like the entire New Testament is not the new covenant.

THE OLD TESTAMENT IS NOT OBSOLETE

The writer of Hebrews repeats Jeremiah's words, saying that with the establishment of the new covenant, the "first" covenant "is becoming obsolete and growing old" and "is ready to vanish away" (8:13). The first covenant spoken of here is not the Old Testament but the Mosaic covenant that God cut with the people of Israel in the wilderness on tablets of stone.

God cut the Mosaic covenant with Israel to *prepare* the Jewish people for the new covenant. The old covenant gave them the law, or God's instruction—it was to be a hedge that would protect them, should they obey everything in it. Unfortunately, man's failure to obey made the Mosaic covenant frail: Israel could not keep God's law and would repeatedly rebel against Him.

The new covenant, which would come later, would eventually replace the Mosaic covenant, just as Jeremiah prophesied. The prophet Ezekiel also prophesied God's law would no longer be written on tablets of stone—He would write it on peoples' hearts:

> Then I will give them one heart, and I will put a new spirit within them, and take the stony heart out of their flesh, and give them a heart of flesh, that they may walk in My statutes and keep My judgments and do them; and they shall be My people, and I will be their God. (Ezekiel 11:19–20; see also Jeremiah 24:7; 32:38–39)

On the first Pentecost after Jesus' ascension, as His disciples waited in the Upper Room in Jerusalem, the Holy Spirit was poured out upon them visibly as tongues of fire (Acts 2:3), and God's law was written on their hearts by the Holy Spirit. The same is true for anyone who believes in Jesus today, as Paul wrote in Romans:

> Even Gentiles, who do not have God's written law, show that they know his law when they instinctively obey it, even without having heard it. They demonstrate that God's law is written in their hearts, for their own conscience and thoughts either accuse them or tell them they are doing right. (2:14–15 NLT)

God fulfilled His promise to once again dwell with man—but this time it was not through a tabernacle or temple. God's presence would dwell in circumcised hearts by the Holy Spirit:

> I will put my dwelling place among you, and I will not abhor you. I will walk among you and be your God, and you will be my people. (Leviticus 26:11–12 NIV)

> My dwelling place will be with them; I will be their God, and they will be my people. (Ezekiel 37:27 NIV)

Jesus Himself cut that covenant, shedding His blood on the tree on our behalf. But God's promise has not been fully implemented—and won't be until Jesus returns. We are in a transitional period where the Mosaic covenant is *becoming* obsolete but is still in place as a covenant that points to our need for the new covenant.

Clearly the entire Old Testament is not what is becoming obsolete. Instead, Hebrews 8:13 references the Mosaic covenant, which is transitioning and will eventually be replaced by the new covenant when it is fully implemented.

JESUS' BIBLE WAS THE OLD TESTAMENT

Anyone promoting disrespect for the Old Testament Scriptures is forgetting the high regard Jesus gave them. First, He never called the Bible "old." What we call the Old Testament today was His Bible, and He referred to it as "the Scriptures" (see Matthew 21:42; 22:29; 26:54; Mark 12:24; 14:49; Luke 24:27, 45).

Jesus often referred directly to the Hebrew Scriptures as well as to the authority behind what was written in them, saying: "It is written ..." For example, when Satan tempted Him in the wilderness, Jesus responded to each temptation by quoting from the Torah, or "the Scriptures"—the Old Testament—alerting us to the supreme value and authority He placed on it for life, thought, and behavior (Matthew 4:4, 7, 10; cf. Deuteronomy 6:13, 16; 8:3).

His entire Sermon on the Mount is taken straight from the Hebrew Scriptures. He also quoted from the Old Testament when He taught about honoring one's parents (see Matthew 15:1–6) and how to obtain eternal life (Matthew 19:16–20).

When the Sadducees questioned Jesus about a particular law in the Old Testament in Matthew 22:23–27, Jesus chastised them using Old Testament Scripture—Exodus 3:6: "Have you not read what was spoken to you by God, saying, 'I am the God of Abraham, and the God of Isaac, and the God of Jacob'? God is not the God of the dead, but of the living" (Matthew 22:31–32; see also Mark 12:26–27; Luke 20:37–38).

Jesus referred to those Scriptures as the Law of Moses, the Prophets, and the Psalms, or sometimes just "the Law and the Prophets":

> Then He said to them, "These are the words which I spoke to you while I was still with you, that all things must be fulfilled which were written in the *Law of Moses and the Prophets and the Psalms* concerning Me." (Luke 24:44, emphasis added; see also Matthew 7:12; 22:40; Luke 16:16)

In this passage, Jesus mentions three sections of Scripture in the Hebrew Bible: the Law (the Torah), the Prophets, and the historical writings (Psalms). Today the Jewish people call their Bible the *Tanakh*. Tanakh stands for the abbreviation *TNK* for the Law (Torah), the Prophets (Nevi'im), and the writings (Ketuvim).

The book of the Torah Jesus quoted most often was Deuteronomy, known in Judaism as the Book of the Law. If Jesus held God's instruction in Deuteronomy in such high regard, we should not disregard it. Jesus believed that the Bible was true and referred to events in the Bible, such as creation, the fall, the flood, and the destruction of Sodom and Gomorrah, as though they actually happened. He also referenced people— such as Abraham, Isaac, and Jacob—as if they existed and even said those

Old Testament heroes are still living.

God spoke to Moses in the burning bush. He fed Israel manna in the desert. And He delivered Jonah from the great fish. Though the stories might sound fantastical, Jesus referred to all these things and more as truth.

PAUL'S BIBLE WAS THE OLD TESTAMENT

Some say that Paul, the apostle to the gentiles, didn't focus on the Old Testament. However, consider Paul's words in his letter to Timothy, one of his disciples:

> *All Scripture* is given by inspiration of God, and is profitable for doctrine, for reproof, for correction, for instruction in righteousness, that the man of God may be complete, thoroughly equipped for every good work. (2 Timothy 3:16–17, emphasis added)

Timothy's mother was Jewish, and his father was Greek. In this passage, Paul affirmed the authority and importance of the Scriptures that Timothy grew up on and knew well. Paul said *all Scripture* was given by inspiration of God.

What Scripture was Paul talking about? The New Testament had not yet been penned, so he was referencing the Hebrew Scriptures—what we call the Old Testament. Paul viewed the Old Testament as the infallible and authoritative word of God.

He often referenced Old Testament passages when affirming that salvation has always been through faith. For example, he wrote in Galatians 3:11 that "No one is justified by the law in the sight of God is evident, for 'the just shall live by faith.'" We might assume that Paul was declaring a New Testament truth in Christ; instead, he was quoting the Old Testament book of Habakkuk: "The just shall live by his faith" (cf. Habakkuk 2:4).

HOW SHOULD WE APPROACH THE OLD TESTAMENT?

Now that we understand the importance of the Old Testament Scriptures, we must discuss *how* to properly approach these ancient writings as we begin to study them. Before reading, studying, and interpreting any verse, passage, or book, consider the following.

The Old Testament Is Divinely Inspired

Second Timothy 3:16 says, "All Scripture is given by *inspiration* of God, and is profitable for doctrine, for reproof, for correction, for instruction in righteousness" (emphasis added). The original Greek for "inspiration" in this verse is *theopneustos*, which means "God-breathed."

Because the Old Testament is God-breathed, inspired by the Creator of the universe, we should approach it with reverence and awe.

The Old Testament Is Also a Human Book

The Hebrew Scriptures are divinely inspired, but as previously mentioned, they are also thoroughly human. Human beings wrote them from their memories, with their words, and with their writing tools (or by dictating to a scribe).

Just as Jesus was fully human and fully divine, we can approach our Bible appreciating the human expression that it is while fully acknowledging it is "God-breathed" and inspired by the Holy Spirit.

The Old Testament Is an Incomplete Account

The Old Testament does not provide a complete account or tell every detail of every story. Instead, it gives details that each writer, under the inspiration of the Holy Spirit, remembered or felt were the most important to include. Because of this, you may have unanswered questions! But because God divinely inspired each author's writing, these details are the ones He wants you to know.

This is why the ancient rabbis extolled the benefits of searching out the Scriptures. Those who care enough to search them out to find answers to their questions will find the hidden riches that await them.

HOW SHOULD WE INTERPRET OLD TESTAMENT SCRIPTURE?

Correctly handling God's Word means we must strive to interpret what it says responsibly—otherwise, we risk misinterpretation and could end up misapplying biblical content. Paul urged his young protégé and ministry partner, Timothy, to "Do your best to present yourself to God as one approved, a worker who does not need to be ashamed and who correctly handles the word of truth" (2 Timothy 2:15 NIV).

The following are some basic principles of sound Bible interpretation. They apply to all Scripture, but here the focus will be specifically on the Old Testament.

Consider Cultural Context

Reading the Bible is a cross-cultural experience. The stories and events in the Old Testament took place within the context of the ancient Middle East and Israel. Because of this, we must be careful not to interpret what we read through the lens of modern Western society.

When studying the Bible, we must consider the details behind the story—things not written, cultural norms of the day, concepts, words, traditions, and issues the authors assumed readers knew. It can be challenging not to interpret a verse through a personal, societal, or cultural lens. But doing so will lead to the wrong interpretation of many events and lessons.

For example, twenty-first-century Westerners are quite individualistic. We're scientific, linear, and logical in how we think. But the Middle Eastern culture in which the biblical stories took place was a group culture that was social and circular instead of linear. It was also relational. This cultural context dramatically impacts how ancient writers told stories.

Unfortunately, we sometimes gloss over this because we tend to approach Scripture from the perspective of the individuals in the story. Consider various aspects of the law. Some laws God gave to Moses make us scratch our heads in confusion. For example, Exodus 21:5–6 tells us if an enslaved person refused freedom, the owner was to pierce their ear with an awl against a doorpost in the presence of witnesses. To our modern minds, this is an odd cultural ceremony!

Without realizing it, we're comparing ancient cultural traditions and law to *today's* society and *today's* practices. And that can lead to misinterpretation.

We must read and interpret unfamiliar practices like this based on the culture and context in which the authors wrote them. When we do, we find that some of the laws we struggle with today were far more advanced than other societies surrounding God's people at that time. God was speaking within the society, culture, and context His people were living in and requiring them to live a degree above that society—to reflect Him and His character to the surrounding nations.

Without a proper understanding of the culture and context of the ancient Middle East, modern Bible readers often miss the depth and richness of details within the biblical stories.

In the same way, Jesus was born into the cultural setting of first-century Israel. He dressed like people back then—He likely wore a tunic and sandals and had a beard and long hair. He certainly spoke their language and was familiar with Middle Eastern culture and first-century societal norms.

If Jesus had talked and dressed the way people dress today, no one would have listened to Him. But He came in ancient biblical times as the Word of God—fully divine, entirely true, and wrapped within the culture and society of *that* day.

So it is with the written Word of God that we call the Bible. It is wrapped in the language and norms of the society in which it was written. For example, when God appeared to Moses and told him to build the tabernacle, He instructed Moses to use animal skins and other materials available to a person in the wilderness 3,500 years ago. By contrast, if God came today and told someone to build a church, He wouldn't ask them to use animal skins. Instead, He'd likely say, "Lay your concrete foundation first. Then frame the building and put siding around it." Likewise, if He tells someone to build a church 2,000 years from now, He won't have them use today's construction materials.

God understands people and their culture and meets them right where they are—according to the time and generation in which they live. That's the wonderful God we serve.

Interpret Contextually

Skeptics will often belittle those who interpret the Bible "literally." But let's be clear about what interpreting the Bible "literally" means: interpreting it according to its literary type and how the authors originally intended it to be understood. It does not mean taking anything out of context, and it certainly does not mean interpreting figurative speech, poetry, or allegory in a literal manner.

Responsible Bible readers interpret Scripture as the original writer intended it to be understood. So, for example, if the genre is poetry, it should be interpreted as poetry. If a passage or story is symbolic, it should be interpreted as allegory. If it's a parable of Jesus, as a parable.

Psalm 62:2 says God is my "rock." Is God really a rock? Of course not! The psalmist meant that God was a place of safety and protection. A literal interpretation would read Psalm 62:2 as the psalmist meant it.

Read with a Timeline Handy

With so many stories and characters—not to mention more than 4,000 years of biblical history—it can be hard to place everything in its proper context, and it's easy to become lost. This is particularly true when reading through the period of the Northern and Southern Kingdoms, each of which had about 20 different kings—it is nearly impossible not to become confused.

Therefore, I advise consulting an Old Testament timeline. The timeline in Appendix A at the back of this book is a helpful tool to have by your side when reading the Old Testament, and it will help you know where you are in the Old Testament story at any time.

Interpret through the Lens of the New Testament
Since the Old Testament was the Bible Jesus, Paul, and the early church used, we must also study their interpretations and applications of the Scriptures. Beyond the original intent of the passage would be how the New Testament writers applied it. They interpreted the Old Testament according to the story of salvation through the Messiah of Israel and His life, death, and resurrection.

THE OLD TESTAMENT, THE FOUNDATION OF OUR FAITH
Interpreting the New Testament without a proper understanding of the Old is like coming into a play at intermission and wondering why we don't understand what's happening or who certain characters are. Everything was set up in the first part of the performance.

Similarly, we won't be able to fully understand the people, stories, and events in the New Testament if we start there. And we won't fully understand who Jesus is and why He came if we begin in Matthew.

The Old Testament is the foundation of the New Testament—and our faith. When we approach it that way, it will enrich our faith and illuminate confusing concepts, stories, and events in the New Testament Scriptures. We will be better disciples because we will more deeply understand who Jesus was and what He taught.

CHAPTER FIVE

The Land of the Bible

*I will multiply your descendants as the stars of heaven;
and all this land that I have spoken of I give to your
descendants, and they shall inherit it forever.*
—*Exodus 32:13*

God's plan to redeem the world is the storyline of the Bible, and central to that plan is God's covenant with Abraham and his descendants, the Jewish people. That covenant includes an inheritance for the children of Israel—a particular piece of real estate.

In Genesis 17:7–8 God described this land as an "everlasting possession" because it was part of the everlasting covenant He made with Abraham. As long as God's covenant with Abraham is in play, the land is Israel's to possess.

Thousands of years later, this piece of land is highly controversial, and some in the Christian world tend to brush its importance aside. They say the land is no longer necessary or that the Jewish people forfeited the right to the land when they did not accept Jesus' messianic credentials.

However, this is far from the truth—there is *profound* significance to the land promised to Abraham and his descendants. But to understand its importance and meaning, we must understand God's original intention in gifting it to the Jewish people.

God promised Abraham in Genesis 12:1–3 that He would make Abraham and his descendants into a great nation. And through that one nation, God would fulfill His eternal plan to redeem the world.

For a group of people to become a nation, they need land: a place to multiply and build their culture, language, institutions, practices, beliefs, and society—everything that makes them a nation. Therefore, land was a critical part of God's covenant that promised Abraham a great nation would come from him.

Just as God needed a people to work through to reach this fallen world, He needed a place from which to do it. The land He chose was, therefore, considered holy—which means "set apart for God's use." God "set aside" the land of Canaan as the place where He would meet with His people and from where He would carry out His great plan of redemption.

A HOLY LAND FOR A HOLY PEOPLE

Though the land was theirs to possess, God was clear: to remain in the land, Israel had to obey and walk righteously before Him. If Israel turned to other gods or rebelled against Him, He would remove them from the land:

> If you do not carefully observe all the words of this law that are written in this book, that you may fear this glorious and awesome name, THE LORD YOUR GOD, then the LORD will bring upon you and your descendants extraordinary plagues—great and prolonged plagues—and serious and prolonged sicknesses. … You shall be left few in number, whereas you were as the stars of heaven in multitude, because you would not obey the voice of the LORD your God. And it shall be, that just as the LORD rejoiced over you to do you good and multiply you, so the LORD will rejoice over you to destroy you and bring you to nothing; and *you shall be plucked from*

off the land which you go to possess. (Deuteronomy 28:58–59, 62–63, emphasis added)

God's punishment for disobedience was harsh because Canaan was no ordinary piece of property. It was to be in this land, on this piece of real estate, that the nation of Israel would live in God's presence. From here, Israel would walk in obedience to His commands and reflect His character to a godless, watching world.

If God's people turned against His presence and offended it, they would tarnish His name—and for that, they would be "plucked from off the land" (Deuteronomy 28:63). The promised land was reserved for a people of faith who wanted to walk in fellowship with their God. It was for a nation that would live its life for the sake of His name and not profane it before other nations.

It was a holy land for a holy people who would live in fellowship with a holy God.

GOD'S STAGE

This unique piece of real estate was also the place from where God would carry out His great plan of redemption. He would not only use the descendants of Abraham, Isaac, and Jacob as the vehicle for causing this to happen, but He would use this land. It would be like a stage, the place from which God would do His mighty works.

After God promised the land to Abraham's descendants, He explained it would be a while before they could possess it because the sins of the current inhabitants had not yet reached the point of judgment:

But in the fourth generation they shall return here, for the iniquity of the Amorites is not yet complete. (Genesis 15:16)

Accordingly, it would be 400 years before Abraham's descendants would take possession of the land of Canaan. In the meantime, though they had grown numerous, they were not yet a nation. They had been enslaved in Egypt and were broken, damaged people with no identity other than that of captive servants.

Before they could possess their promised land, they had to meet this God who had freed them from bondage and commit to walking in obedience to Him. This was the intent of the Mosaic covenant, which was more like a marriage proposal. The people of Israel agreed to be God's children—and He would be their God.

Only then was Israel able to possess the land, and over the next few hundred years, God's people grew into a mighty nation with a king, language, society, and culture. God revealed His character and law to them and directed them through the Hebrew prophets. Their priests maintained the ancient writings of those prophets as well as the writings of Moses.

But all of this had to be put on hold once God's people fell into persistent idolatry and betrayed Him. They had acted like an unfaithful wife, and as He had warned them from the beginning—before they had even arrived in Canaan or established Jerusalem—they had to be banished from the land.

The first exile was short-lived, and after 70 years, the people were allowed to return and rebuild their temple and the walls of the city of Jerusalem. Five hundred years later, and in the fulness of time, Jesus—the promised Messiah—was born. His ministry focused on revealing the Father to His children, the house of Israel. At the end of Jesus' life, He paid the price for sin on the cross, just as Isaiah had foreseen (see Isaiah 53). But while Jesus won the forgiveness of sins for anyone who would believe in Him, the full implementation of the kingdom of God would come much later.

In the meantime, the children of Israel persisted in deep divisiveness and their leaders in political corruption, resulting in a second exile—this one much longer. And for the next 1,900 years, generations of Jews prayed that "next year" they would be back in Jerusalem.

Profoundly, Isaiah 11:11 had predicted a second return to the land. That return began in the late 1800s as Jews from the north, south, east, and west started to make their way back to their promised land. By 1948 the Jewish people had declared statehood in the same land God had promised them through Abraham. (We'll explore this idea of a second return in more detail in chapter 6.)

Today, as world events spiral out of control, it looks as though God is setting the stage for the culmination of all history. Rabbis refer to this return as the "dawn of redemption." God's birthing people are back in their land. We are just waiting for the curtain to lift and the final act to begin.

WHY THE LAND OF CANAAN?

The land God chose to be His stage for this magnificent story was called the land of Canaan because it had been inhabited by the Canaanites, the descendants of Canaan. Canaan was a son of Ham, who was a son of Noah.

However, even though they had once inhabited the land, God called Canaan "my" land in 2 Chronicles 7:20 (see also Leviticus 25:23). As the owner, He has every right to do with it as He wants. He owns the deed to the real estate and gave this particular property to Israel. Recall that God had said to Abraham:

> Get out of your country, from your family and from your father's house, to a land that I will show you. I will make you a great nation; I will bless you and make your name great; and you shall be a blessing. I will bless those who bless you, and I will curse him who curses you; and in you all the families of the earth shall be blessed. *So Abram departed* as the Lord had spoken to him. (Genesis 12:1–4, emphasis added)

Notice that Abraham believed God, packed up, and left his country to follow the Lord to a foreign land. He obeyed and acted by faith (see Hebrews 11:8).

But then in Genesis 15:8, Abraham questioned how he would know he and his descendants would inherit the land. In verse 18 God responded by confirming His promise with a covenant: "On the same day the LORD made ("cut"; in Hebrew *kārat*) a covenant with [Abraham], saying: 'To your descendants I have given this land.'"

This covenant—promised in Genesis 12:1–3 and "cut" in Genesis 15:18—sets aside people and land for the blessing of the nations: "In you [Abraham] all the families of the earth shall be blessed" (Genesis 12:3). Centuries later in Galatians 3:8, the apostle Paul would refer to this covenant as one of the earliest proclamations of the gospel:

> And the Scripture, foreseeing that God would justify the Gentiles by faith, preached the gospel to Abraham beforehand, saying, "In you all the nations shall be blessed."

In his article "Israel and the Enduring Land Promise," Rev. Malcolm Hedding calls the Abrahamic covenant "the great covenant of the Bible" because it promises salvation to a world lost in sin. He writes:

> It is, therefore, "the covenant of decision," and all the other great covenants of the Bible flow out of it. The Jewish people, as Abraham's descendants, are chosen as the servants of the covenant. In other words, the nation of Israel is not brought into existence as an end to itself but as a means to an end—the salvation of the world. They are the means by which God delivers His redemptive initiative to the world.[7]

---

[7] Malcolm Hedding, "Israel and the Enduring Land Promise," International Christian Embassy Jerusalem, 2013.

Thus, the land of Canaan is the unique, holy piece of land God chose for Abraham and his descendants and from where God would perform His great redemptive acts on Earth.

WHY JERUSALEM?

God not only chose a piece of property as His stage, but He also set apart a particular city. He repeatedly says that out of the entire earth, Jerusalem is where He will place His name. In Deuteronomy, when the Israelites were in the wilderness and God was giving them the law and telling them how to worship according to His legal requirements, He said seven different times, "And when you go to worship in the place that I will choose—" do this and that. Consider just three of those verses:

> But you shall seek *the place where the LORD your God chooses*, out of all your tribes, *to put His name for His dwelling place*; and there you shall go. (Deuteronomy 12:5, emphasis added)

> Then there will be *the place where the LORD your God chooses to make His name abide*. There you shall bring all that I command you: your burnt offerings, your sacrifices, your tithes, the heave offerings of your hand, and all your choice offerings which you vow to the LORD. (Deuteronomy 12:11, emphasis added)

> Therefore you shall sacrifice the Passover to the LORD your God, from the flock and the herd, *in the place where the LORD chooses to put His name*. (Deuteronomy 16:2, emphasis added)

Almost 400 years later, God revealed that the "place" He wanted them to worship Him was Jerusalem. In 2 Chronicles 6:6, David's son, Solomon, recounted how God had said: "I have chosen Jerusalem, that My name may be there, and I have chosen David to be over My people Israel." The below verses affirm Jerusalem was indeed the place God chose for His name to dwell forever:

> And Rehoboam the son of Solomon reigned in Judah. Rehoboam was forty-one years old when he became king. He reigned seventeen years *in Jerusalem, the city which the LORD had chosen out of all the tribes of Israel, to put His name there.* (1 Kings 14:21, emphasis added)

> And to his son I will give one tribe, that My servant David may always have a lamp before Me *in Jerusalem, the city which I have chosen for Myself, to put My name there.* (1 Kings 11:36, emphasis added)

> He built altars in the house of the LORD, of which the LORD had said, *"In Jerusalem I will put My name."* (2 Kings 21:4, emphasis added)

Later, when Solomon built the temple in Jerusalem, God said:

> For now I have chosen and sanctified this house, that My name may be there forever; and My eyes and My heart will be there perpetually. (2 Chronicles 7:16)

LOCATION, LOCATION, LOCATION

God chose the land of Canaan and the city of Jerusalem. And for some people, that's all they need to know! But others have questions: "Well, why there? Why that piece of land?"

Unfortunately, the Bible doesn't explain why God chose that particular city or piece of land. However, many Bible teachers have pointed out that the land of Canaan was strategic because of its location on the land bridge between three continents: Europe, Asia, and Africa. This unique location means Canaan was the front line of battles between the major empires ruling those three continents. Many empires have taken over the land of Israel throughout the years—one army from the north, the next one from the south, the Greeks from the west. Other nations' militaries were continually invading Israel while on their way somewhere. It was a dangerous place.

But it could be that God strategically placed the Jewish people on this piece of land to be a light to the nations passing by. They were located along major trade routes and should have been like a city on a hill shining brightly into darkness for many to see and be drawn to. They were perfectly positioned to reflect the holiness of their God to the nations.

During the Roman Empire, this traffic increased due to the vast network of Roman roads. Sea traffic also swelled, thanks to Herod the Great's man-made port of Caesarea. After Jesus' death, resurrection, and ascension, the gospel easily spread from here throughout the world.

There's also a more mysterious possibility for this location. Though the Bible doesn't say this, some rabbis have suggested Jerusalem could be the same location as the garden of Eden. The Bible only tells us the garden was near four rivers (see Genesis 2:8–14). We know where two of those rivers are today (both the Euphrates and the *Hiddekel* [Tigris] Rivers' headwaters originate in modern-day Turkey; see v. 14) but not the other two. It is possible the garden of Eden—and the description of these rivers—was from a time before two of the rivers dried up or became parts of larger seas when land masses moved.

We do not know. But in God's sight Jerusalem is in the center of the world: "This is what the Sovereign LORD says: This is Jerusalem, which I have set in the center of the nations, with countries all around her" (Ezekiel 5:5 NIV).

Rabbinic tradition holds that God created Adam on the very rock on Mount Moriah where the holy of holies later stood, the same place Abraham took his son, Isaac, to sacrifice him. Ancient Jerusalem is where Abraham met the mysterious priest and king, Melchizedek, who was there worshiping the One True God (see Genesis 14:18). Some say Melchizedek is a type of Christ. Others say he's just a king who worshiped God (Hebrews 7:3, 8). We don't know for sure who this person was, but we do know He was king of Salem (Jerusalem) and that he blessed Abraham:

> Then Melchizedek king of Salem brought out bread and wine; he was the priest of God Most High. And he blessed him and said: "Blessed be [Abraham] of God Most High, possessor of heaven and earth; and blessed be God Most High, who has delivered your enemies into your hand." And he gave him a tithe of all. (Genesis 14:18–20)

> For this Melchizedek, king of Salem, priest of the Most High God, who met Abraham returning from the slaughter of the kings and blessed him, to whom also Abraham gave a tenth part of all, first being translated "king of righteousness," and then also king of Salem, meaning "king of peace." (Hebrews 7:1–2)

Interestingly, even topography supports God's identification of this place where He placed His name. Jerusalem has three valleys that come together to make the Hebrew letter "shin" or ש, which looks a bit like the English letter W.

The Hebrew letter *shin* stands both for *Shaddai* in God's name *El Shaddai* and for "name." For example, in Hebrew, *Ha Shem* or "the name" is how Jews today refer to God. Notice that "shem" (שם) starts with the letter *shin* (ש, reading right to left).

Quite literally, God has written His name into the topography of Jerusalem.

Clearly, there's an eternal significance to the land and the city of Jerusalem, and the Bible doesn't fully explain it. But we can take what we do have, let Scripture interpret Scripture, and try to understand it as best we can.

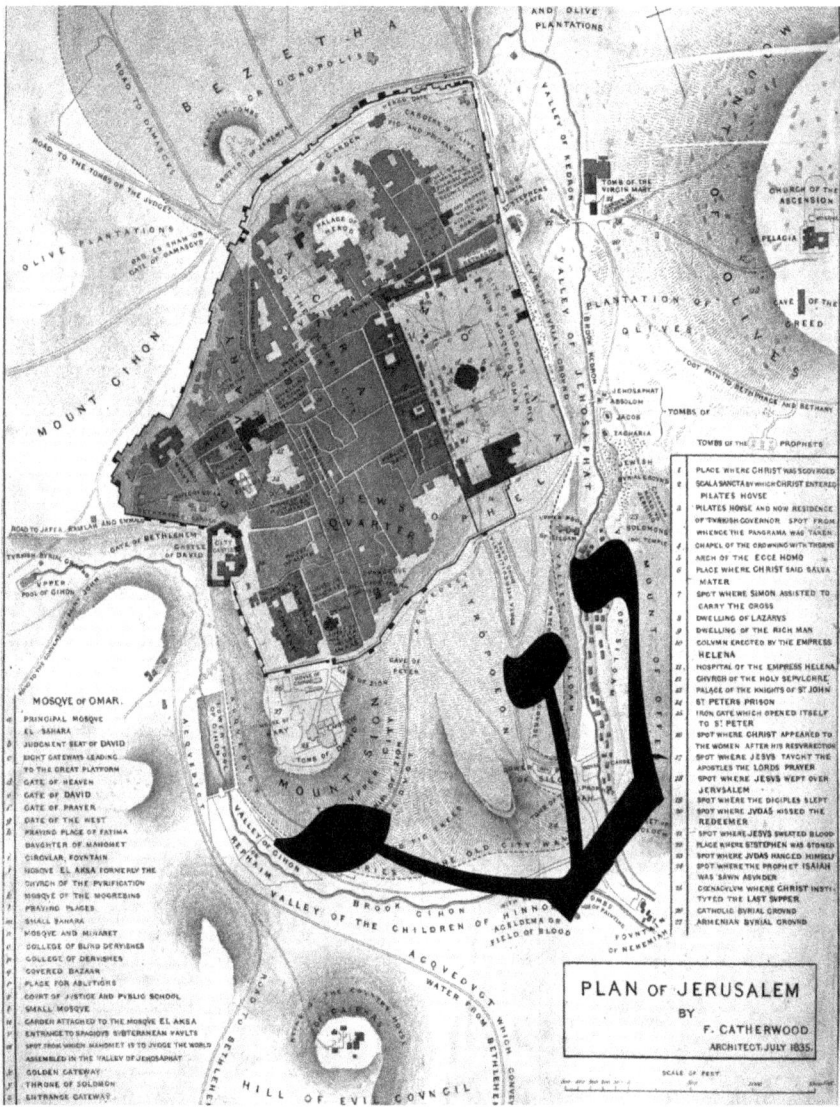

Image of the three valleys that comprise the city of Jerusalem's geography, making the Hebrew letter "shin" or ש, which stands for God's name. Frederick Catherwood, *Plan of Jerusalem*, 1835 (source: commons.wikimedia.com).

A PLACE OF TESTING

Even though God promised this special place to the children of Israel as their eternal inheritance (Genesis 13:15), it required faith for them to enter Canaan. While still in the wilderness, Moses sent 12 spies to scout the land before taking it. Ten returned with a negative report.

But two men, Joshua and Caleb, returned full of confidence, declaring Israel should go up at once and take possession, for their God would give them the land:

> The land we passed through to spy out is an exceedingly good land. If the LORD delights in us, then He will bring us into this land and give it to us, "a land which flows with milk and honey." Only do not rebel against the LORD, nor fear the people of the land, for they are our bread; their protection has departed from them, and the LORD is with us. Do not fear them. (Numbers 14:7–9)

Sadly, because of the unbelief of the majority who had sided with the 10, God allowed the Israelites to wander for 40 years in the desert until that entire generation died except for Joshua and Caleb. It would be Joshua who would lead the next generation into the promised land.

Without faith, Joshua and Caleb would never have entered the land. Instead, they would have stayed where they thought it was safe, in the desert, where God provided manna every day.

The promised land would be a place of testing for this new generation of Israelites. Even though it was a land "flowing with milk and honey" (Exodus 3:17)—a phrase implying it was a rich land of abundance—entering Canaan required a tremendous amount of faith and obedience because taking possession of it would not come without challenges.

First, there were giants in the land. Upon their return from scouting out the land, the spies told Moses:

"We went to the land where you sent us. It truly flows with milk and honey, and this is its fruit. Nevertheless the people who dwell in the land are strong; the cities are fortified and very large; moreover we saw the descendants of Anak there. The Amalekites dwell in the land of the South; the Hittites, the Jebusites, and the Amorites dwell in the mountains; and the Canaanites dwell by the sea and along the banks of the Jordan. ... We are not able to go up against the people, for they are stronger than we." And they gave the children of Israel a bad report of the land which they had spied out, saying, "The land through which we have gone as spies is a land that devours its inhabitants, and all the people whom we saw in it are men of great stature. *There we saw the giants* (the descendants of Anak came from the giants); and we were like grasshoppers in our own sight, and so we were in their sight." (Numbers 13:27–29, 31–33, emphasis added)

Moses confirmed that the spies weren't exaggerating. In Deuteronomy 9:1–2, just before Israel was to cross the Jordan, he told the Israelites they were to "go in to dispossess nations greater and mightier than [themselves], cities great and fortified up to heaven, *a people great and tall, the descendants of the Anakim*" (emphasis added).[8]

In addition, after they crossed the Jordan River (just before taking Jericho and then the rest of the land), the Israelites faced an extensive line of rocky, barren, dry cliffs. Nevertheless, after considerable challenges and trials, they pressed on and took the lush land God had promised them through Abraham—by faith.

---

[8] The Anakim (also called "Anakites") were a race of giant people (see Deuteronomy 2:10, 21; 9:2) who lived in ancient Southern Israel before the Israelites arrived. The Anakim can be traced to Anak, Arba's son (Joshua 15:13; 21:11); Joshua 14:15 refers to Arba as "the greatest man among the Anakim."

THE LAND—A TYPE OR SHADOW

In God's grand narrative of the Bible, He has included what the theological world calls "types and shadows" or "typology." Typology is a special kind of symbolism where a person or thing—something in the natural world in the Old Testament—represents or "foreshadows" a spiritual principle in the New Testament.

The New Testament affirms this concept. For example, Paul wrote that the Old Testament feasts (also called "festivals"; see Leviticus 23), new moon celebrations, and sabbaths "are a *shadow* of things to come" (Colossians 2:17, emphasis added).

The promised land is also an example of this kind of symbolism. The land Israel entered was a real, literal piece of property. But that was only the shadow. Through Jesus ("Yeshua," in Hebrew, which interestingly is another pronunciation of "Joshua"), we can enter the "land," our salvation, and enjoy all Christ won for us on the cross. Like the Israelites under Joshua's leadership, it takes faith to "enter in," defeat our enemies, and possess the "land."

The promised land is a profound type and shadow of salvation and our need for faith. But it is also a type and shadow of our need to be obedient and walk in fellowship with God so that we might overcome all hindrances and enjoy the abundance of the great salvation He has purchased for us.

A LAND OF CONTRASTS

The land of Israel is also full of geographic contrasts rich in spiritual lessons. Recall that God gave each tribe of Israel an allotment of land, a different territory. Each piece of land was dramatically different from the others, which meant each tribe had its challenges and opportunities for abundance

On the map showing Israel's tribal allocations, notice that the northernmost tribes are Asher and Naphtali. At the northern tip of

Naphtali is the ancient city of Dan. Farther north than Dan is a mountain called Mount Hermon, the highest point in Israel today. The elevation is so high Mount Hermon receives substantial snowfall—so much so that Israelis today enjoy skiing on the mountain. The headwaters of the Jordan river begin in the mountainous region around Dan.

Map of territories allotted to the 12 tribes of Israel (source: commons.wikimedia.org)

Just below Mount Hermon is a mountain range running due south known as the Golan Heights. To the west are the mountains extending down from Lebanon into the area of Asher. In the middle of those two mountain ranges is the beautiful Hula Valley—lush farmland.

The Hula Valley in Israel with Mount Hermon in the background
(source: commons.wikimedia.org)

A little to the south of the Hula Valley is the Sea of Galilee, the lowest freshwater sea (or lake) on Earth. To its west is the mountainous Galilee region, which also includes the large, fertile Jezreel Valley.

The Jordan River runs south from the Sea of Galilee along what is called the Jordan Valley—a long and narrow trough running all the way to the Dead Sea that is also a rift between the African and Asian plates. The gap between those two continental plates makes it the lowest place on Earth.

View of the Sea of Galilee and the Golan Heights (source: commons.wikimedia.org)

The north part of the Jordan Valley (source: commons.wikimedia.org)

To the west of the Jordan Valley is a mountainous, hilly area called "the wilderness." It is a rocky, barren desert with dry, sharp cliffs where nothing grows—and at the same time, it is majestic, unlike any other place in the world. At the western edge of that barren wilderness, the city of Jerusalem rises, dividing that barren plateau to its east from the fertile rolling hills on its west that lead down to the Mediterranean Sea. It takes only an hour-and-a-half to drive from the Mediterranean Sea up to the mountains through Jerusalem into that barren wasteland and then down to the lowest place on Earth at the Jordan River. Israel is incredibly diverse and offers impressive, colorful, and unique landscapes for such a small piece of land.

Judean wilderness (source: commons.wikimedia.org)

Its extremes provide everything from lush gardens with roaring waterfalls to rocky, barren deserts that seldom see rain. Many of these landscapes reflect scenes in living color of poetic writings in the Bible. For example, nothing compares to sitting in the barren Judean wilderness below the Ein Gedi waterfall (pictured on the cover of this book) and reading some of the Psalms—particularly those David wrote while hiding

The hills surrounding the modern city of Jerusalem (source: commons.wikimedia.org)

from King Saul in that area (see 1 Samuel 21–24). David's description of the deer panting for streams of water in Psalm 42:1 comes to life each evening when herds of mountain goats make their way to the Ein Gedi springs for water. His description of God as his rock and refuge is also vividly understood here. Towering above the springs and waterfall are mountainous cliffs filled with caves just like the ones David found refuge in.

The writer of Psalm 125 was obviously sitting on a hillside outside of Jerusalem when he compared God's protection to the mountains surrounding the city:

As the mountains surround Jerusalem, so the LORD surrounds His people from this time forth and forever. (Psalm 125:2)

While Jerusalem is seated on a hill, higher mountains indeed surround it. What a beautiful portrayal of God surrounding His people

An ariel view of the Mount of Olives and the hills surrounding Jerusalem

and watching over them. Israel is God's land, and Jerusalem is the city that He chose to place His name—the one identified city in the world from where His presence and blessings would flow.

And while we know we can pray to God from anywhere, and He is not bound to any location, there is something to be said for the past, future, and eternal significance of this land. That is why Isaiah called on everyone who knows the Lord and prays to be watchmen on the walls of Jerusalem:

> I have set watchmen on your walls, O Jerusalem; they shall never hold their peace day or night. You who make mention of the LORD, do not keep silent, and give Him no rest till He establishes and till He makes Jerusalem a praise in the earth. (Isaiah 62:6–7)

CHAPTER SIX

The People of the Bible

He will set up a banner for the nations, and will assemble the outcasts of Israel, and gather together the dispersed of Judah from the four corners of the earth.
—Isaiah 11:12

The Bible references three prominent groups of people, and it is critical to understand who those groups are, what applies to which one, and where they differ: Israel, the church, and the nations. Interestingly, Jesus' final words to His disciples in Acts 1 refer to *all three groups.*

After Jesus was crucified and resurrected, He spent 40 days with the disciples teaching them about the kingdom of God (Acts 1:3). Then, just before He ascended to heaven from the Mount of Olives, His disciples asked:

> "Lord, will You at this time restore the kingdom to Israel?" And He said to them, "It is not for you to know times or seasons which the Father has put in His own authority. But you shall receive power when the Holy Spirit has come upon you; and you shall be witnesses to Me in Jerusalem, and in all Judea and Samaria, and to the end of the earth." (Acts 1:6–8)

The disciples' question may sound like it was coming out of left field: *How could the disciples have spent so much time with Jesus and then asked such a question?* We almost expect Jesus to rebuke them for not understanding that God's kingdom is spiritual and not of this world.

Instead, Jesus responded that the timing of the restoration of the kingdom to Israel was not for them to know. He did not deny that it would happen—He simply addressed the issue of timing. He then proceeded to commission them as the church to receive the power of the Holy Spirit and be a witness for Him "to the end of the earth."

In this one passage, we see the contrasting roles of Israel and the church side by side. We see God's calling on Israel and His promise of future physical restoration *and* the calling on the church to go out into the world and preach the good news of the gospel to the nations. Though distinct, they function side by side with the same end goal: to reach the nations—fallen humankind.

Let's begin by exploring God's calling on Israel.

ISRAEL'S CALLING

As discussed in previous chapters, the story of the Bible is the story of God's plan to redeem the world, and central to that story is the Jewish people and their calling to live in a particular land—Israel—and be the vehicle of God's redemptive plan in the earth. God chose this people group "above all the peoples on the face of the earth" as His "special treasure" (Deuteronomy 7:6; see also Psalm 135:4).

Unfortunately, in today's culture, there tends to be an aversion to the idea of any one people group being what we would call "exceptional." When it comes to the "chosen-ness" of the Jewish people (Scripture often refers to the Jews as God's chosen people; see Deuteronomy 14:2; Isaiah 43:10; and others), identifying one people group as "chosen" can seem arrogant and even offensive.

To be clear, God did not line up all the peoples of the earth and say,

"Okay, I like this people group better than the rest, so I'm going to work with them." God needed people to work through, so He *created* the nation of Israel for this purpose. He chose Abraham and said, "I will make you into a great nation." Though Abraham's wife, Sarah, was barren, she miraculously conceived Isaac, and the nation was born.

God told Abraham that anyone who blessed his descendants would be blessed because blessing the Jewish people would be supporting God's choice and plan—they would be siding with Him. They would be assisting in the blessing and even survival of the Jewish people. God always intended there to be non-Jewish people who would love, bless, and help His people. It was part of His plan.

In return, gentiles are blessed by the redemptive products given to us through the Jewish people. We partake of salvation through the Jewish Messiah, the covenants, the promises, and God's law. The entire Bible we study today exists because they protected and preserved the Scriptures. Everything Christians hold dear comes from the Jewish people. We are indeed blessed.

A PEOPLE WHO WOULD SUFFER

However, this calling to be the vehicle of God's redemptive plan would not be easy—the Jewish people would experience great opposition and tremendous suffering carrying out their charge. Several decades after Jesus' death, John penned what we know today as the book of Revelation. And through apocalyptic imagery in Revelation, John vividly affirmed the calling of the Jewish people and the spiritual forces arrayed against them.

In Revelation 12:1–2, John saw Israel as a woman clothed with the sun and the moon with 12 stars around her head, which symbolizes the 12 tribes of Israel. The woman was pregnant and about to birth a Child—she was in labor and experiencing great pain. Sitting in front of her was an evil dragon:

> Behold, a great, fiery red dragon having seven heads and ten horns, and seven diadems on his heads. His tail drew a third of the stars of

heaven and threw them to the earth. And *the dragon stood before the woman who was ready to give birth*, to devour her Child as soon as it was born. (Revelation 12:3–4, emphasis added)

The woman bore the male Child, whom John said in verse 5 was "to rule the nations with a rod of iron." This male Child is the Messiah. The woman's Child was caught up to heaven, and the woman fled into the wilderness where she was kept safe in "a place prepared by God" (v. 6). John then described a great war against the woman and her offspring:

And the dragon was enraged with the woman, and he went to make war with the rest of her offspring, who keep the commandments of God and have the testimony of Jesus Christ. (v. 17)

The spiritual attack was against the male Child, whom the dragon (Satan) tried unsuccessfully to destroy. So he turned his attention to the woman (Israel) and then to her offspring. His tactic? Destroy the woman (Israel) because if he could eradicate her, God's plan of redemption through her would end.

It's as if Satan is thinking: *If I can keep the Jewish people off the land and wipe them out, then all of God's promises and plans will not come to pass.*

This woman (Israel) who birthed the Messiah has been incessantly persecuted for centuries and continues to be persecuted today. Yet God has kept her safe, so the "dragon" has turned his attention to her other offspring: Christians—those who have the "testimony of Jesus." Christians have suffered persecution from the very beginning, but today they are the most persecuted religious group on Earth. More martyrs have died for their faith in the last century than in all previous centuries combined.

Interestingly, Revelation 12 also indicates *why* Satan will attack Christians: we have the testimony of the male Child he hates. We are called to take that testimony to the nations, and he wants to stop us. We will discuss this calling in more detail later in this chapter but for now, let's continue with our discussion of the calling of Israel.

AN EVIL PLAN TO DESTROY ISRAEL

Another Scripture that portrays Satan's evil pursuit of the people of Israel is in Psalm 83:

> O God! ... Those who hate You ... have taken crafty counsel against Your people, and consulted together against Your sheltered ones. They have said, "Come, and *let us cut them off from being a nation, that the name of Israel may be remembered no more.*" (vv. 1–4, emphasis added)

The psalmist was clear: God's enemies hate His people and have devised an evil plan to destroy them. It is a spiritual war against God Himself, and His people are in the line of fire. They must be annihilated to destroy God's plan because at the end of the day, His plan results in the demise of the evil forces arrayed against Him.

The history of the Jewish people reveals Satan's ongoing evil pursuit of them, which defies explanation. It is irrational, and it is spiritual at its root. It has come to be known as antisemitism. The following are examples of its persistence from generation to generation and from one place to the next.

Haman

The biblical story of Esther takes place in the setting of the Persian Empire in the fifth century BC before the time of Jesus. King Cyrus of Persia had conquered Babylon and allowed the Jews to return to Jerusalem, effectively ending their 70 years of exile in Babylon. The Persian king at the time of Esther was King Ahasuerus, who scholars agree is the same King Xerxes who appears in other historical sources.

Esther's cousin, Mordecai, refused to bow down to the king's second-in-command, Haman. Infuriated by Mordecai's resolve, Haman began plotting the annihilation of all the Jews in the Persian Empire. At that time, the Persian Empire extended from India in the east to Ethiopia in the west, which was most of the known world. If Haman had succeeded in eradicating all the Jews in the empire, it would have meant the end of the Jewish people altogether.

Esther risked her life and went before the king to reveal Haman's evil plot. The king then ordered Haman to be hung on the very gallows Haman intended to hang Mordecai. Not only were the Jews preserved, but the king allowed the Jews to defend themselves against their enemies.

While the story of Esther might be familiar, few realize its significance. The threat to the "Jews of Persia" was a threat to the survival of the Jewish people—period. The Persian Empire was so large it encompassed almost all the Jews at the time. Had Haman's plan succeeded, the entire nation of Israel would have ceased to exist. Joseph and Mary would never have been born to one day birth and raise Jesus, and the biblical story of salvation would have ended.

Antiochus Epiphanes

Because the Jews were bound to observe the Law of Moses and were forbidden to worship other gods, they were often considered rebellious (or at least disrespectful) regarding the pagan worship most emperors required. This was especially evident when Greek rulers sought to force Greek culture and its pagan worship—known as Hellenization—upon conquered lands. The Jews would not and could not participate.

The Persian Empire had been defeated by Alexander the Great, and successive Greek rulers sought to impose Hellenization to secure control of the population. When Seleucid King Antiochus IV Epiphanes decided to force the worship of pagan gods on the Jewish people to unify the religions of the regions, the situation grew ugly. In 167 BC he turned the Jewish Temple into a syncretic Greek-Jewish cult, complete with an altar to Zeus. He also sacrificed an abominable animal (probably a pig) on the altar of burnt offerings. According to Jewish law, these acts defiled the temple.

Eventually (and miraculously), Jewish Zealots, led by the Jewish priest Mattathias and his sons, defeated the Greek forces, cleansed the temple, and rededicated it. In the New Testament the commemoration of this event was called the Feast of Dedication, more commonly known today as Hannukah or the "Festival of Lights."

While it is debatable whether this story is an example of antisemitism or simply a clash of cultures, it demonstrates how people hated the Jews for their obedience to God, which set them apart from other people.

The Roman Empire

The Roman Empire also came to hate the Jews. Several rebellions against the brutal Roman occupation in the first and second centuries led to the temple's destruction and the Jews being expelled from the land and dispersed throughout the known world. The Roman emperor Hadrian made Jerusalem a pagan city by erecting a statue of Zeus in a rebuilt temple and renaming the city Aelia Capitolina, while he renamed Judea "Palestine."

Though many Jews lost their lives at the hands of the Romans, God preserved the Jewish people among the nations.

Islam

The religion of Islam originated in Arabia in the seventh century AD. As Islam expanded, it took over the former land of Israel. Jews who refused to convert to Islam or agree to become *dhimmis* (second-class citizens) were often killed. When people become dhimmis, both then and now, they are allowed to practice their religion, but many times in history, they were required to pay a high tax for this luxury. Whether they were killed, converted, or became dhimmis, the intended consequence was the elimination of the Jewish people—at least as Jews.

Despite these efforts, Jews survived; over the centuries, some even fared well in Islamic lands. Others fled west to areas such as Spain.

The Spanish Inquisition

The Jewish community thrived in Spain and had become the largest in the world by the fifteenth century. However, even though Spain was religiously and ethnically diverse, with Jews, Christians, and Muslims living in the same regions, the newly unified kingdom desired religious unity. So in 1478 Pope Sixtus IV issued a decree authorizing Catholic monarchs King Ferdinand II and Queen Isabella I to root out heresy in the Spanish kingdoms and rid the region of people not part of the Catholic Church—and they did so through brutal means.

Unfortunately, Spain's Jewish population became a target. In 1492 the monarchs issued a decree giving Jews four months to convert to Christianity or leave the kingdom. Those who stayed had to convert, or they were imprisoned or killed.

The Spanish Inquisition would continue for 350 years. Most Spanish Jews were either converted, wiped out, or exiled to other countries where they survived. Unfortunately, wherever they migrated, they encountered antisemitism and the threat of more expulsions. Large communities of Jews made their way to Latin America, and others made their way east and began growing in Poland and surrounding areas where they were allowed to settle.

Russian Pogroms

From 1881 to 1884 more than 200 anti-Jewish riots called "pogroms" occurred in the Russian Empire, triggered by the assassination of Czar Alexander II. Some had blamed "agents of foreign influence" for Alexander's death, implying the Jews were at fault. These exaggerated claims reinforced the antisemitic leanings of the largely Russian Orthodox

Czars, which led to these pogroms that swept through southwestern Imperial Russia (present-day Ukraine and Poland), a story highlighted in the movie *Fiddler on the Roof*.

However, there was a silver lining: these Russian pogroms emboldened several waves of Jews to make their way to their ancient homeland, Israel, to build agricultural communities and start new lives.

The Holocaust

At the beginning of the twentieth century, the largest community of Jews lived in Europe, where they enjoyed a rich and diverse set of cultures developed over their 2,000-year presence there. Most Jews in prewar Europe lived in Eastern Europe, with about 3,000,000 Jews in Poland, 2,525,000 in the Soviet Union, and 756,000 in Romania.[9] The largest population of Jews in central Europe lived in Germany, about 525,000, followed by Hungary with 445,000.[10] In addition, approximately 300,000 Jews lived in Great Britain and about 73,000 in Greece.

But in just a decade, most of Europe would be conquered, occupied, or annexed by Nazi Germany and its Axis partners. Nazi ideology considered Jews to be an inferior race and, as such, endangered the purity and strength of the Aryan race. Thus, the Nazi regime embarked on a program to annihilate the Jews, shipping off millions of men, women, and children to concentration camps, where most were eventually killed. One million Jews died at Auschwitz alone.

At the end of the Holocaust in 1945, at least six million Jews—two out of every three European Jews—were dead. Yet as devastating as this was to the Jewish community, many survived, and some went on to build large and successful communities in the United States and Israel.

---

[9] United States Holocaust Museum, "Jewish Population in Europe in 1933: Population Data by Country," (Washington, DC).
[10] United States Holocaust Museum, "Jewish."

Modern Antisemitism

Antisemitism is rising at alarming rates around the world, making it increasingly dangerous for Jews in almost every country. The largest Jewish community today is in Israel, so the long saga of Jew-hatred now has an anti-Israel chapter currently being written. This political expression of antisemitism—anti-Zionism—seeks to turn the global community against and bring an end to the Jewish State. Israel is also under a serious threat of annihilation by Iran, which regularly threatens to destroy Israel while working to develop the nuclear weapons required to do so.

Time after time throughout history, the Jewish people have been threatened with destruction. But despite the suffering Israel would experience, God promised He would protect His people:

> Whoever assembles against you [Israel] shall fall for your sake. ...
> No weapon formed against you shall prosper. (Isaiah 54:15, 17)

> Those who strive with you [Israel] shall perish. (Isaiah 41:11)

> I ... will be a wall of fire around her [Israel]. (Zechariah 2:5)

In the nineteenth century, the German Kaiser asked German Chancellor Bismarck: "Bismarck, can you prove the existence of God?" Bismarck responded, "The Jews, your majesty. The Jews." Despite centuries of antisemitism, God's promise in Jeremiah 31:36 that Israel would never cease to be a nation before Him has proven to be true.

Israel Is God's Banner to the Nations

The Jews have survived centuries of persecution solely because of God's hand of protection over them. In our day, we can see they have not only survived but thrived—*and* returned home to the same land promised to them through Abraham. There is no explanation for this except a biblical one.

Recall that in chapter 3, we talked about how God would bring Israel back to the land a second time. After their 70-year captivity in Babylon, the gentile King Cyrus allowed the Jews to return to their land and rebuild their temple (their first exile and first return). But after Rome sacked Jerusalem in AD 70, the Jews were exiled a second time—this time throughout the known world. Jews have been scattered from one end of the earth to the other ever since.

The modern-day Jewish return to the land is the second return. Let's revisit a familiar verse in Isaiah:

> In that day the Lord will reach out his hand *a second time* to reclaim the surviving remnant of his people from Assyria, from Lower Egypt, from Upper Egypt, from Cush, from Elam, from Babylonia, from Hamath and from the islands of the Mediterranean. (Isaiah 11:11 NIV, emphasis added)

Notice that Isaiah's prophecy of this second return is not just from one nation—as in the first return from Babylon—but from many nations. But then, in verse 12, there is a profound detail not to miss:

> He will set up a *banner for the nations*, and will assemble the outcasts of Israel, and gather together the dispersed of Judah from the four corners of the earth. (Isaiah 11:12, emphasis added)

In this return, Isaiah said God will raise a banner (some translations say "ensign" or "flag") to the nations. In the original Hebrew, the word for "banner" is *nēs*, which means "Something lifted up, a standard, a signal, or a sign." A "banner" often signaled victory in a battle. In Isaiah 11:12, God's act of setting up a "banner for the nations" may carry a twofold message to the nations that is both positive and negative.

God Is Faithful to His Word

First, seeing Israel return to the land a second time affirms God's victorious power and His great faithfulness. This return, which is nothing short of a miracle, is a rallying call to the nations to get on board—God is on the move! Believers worldwide are rejoicing in God's faithfulness to the Jewish people, knowing that if He keeps His promises to Israel, He will keep *all* His promises.

The regathering of the exiles is a "banner" (sign) for believers that God is mighty and victorious, and we can trust Him because He is faithful and true to His word. What an awesome show of God's power and goodness for all to see and be drawn to.

God Will Judge Nations That Oppose Israel

However, for nations opposed to God and what He is doing, God's banner is also a warning: He will fulfill His promise to protect Israel and bring her home, but He will also keep His promise of a coming day of reckoning for those nations that oppose her. In Joel 3 God makes this warning to Israel's enemies clear:

> For behold, in those days and at that time, when I bring back the captives of Judah and Jerusalem, I will also gather all nations, and bring them down to the Valley of Jehoshaphat; and I will enter into judgment with them there on account of My people, My heritage Israel, whom they have scattered among the nations; they have also divided up My land. (vv. 1–2)

Judgment *will* come to the nations that have treated the Jewish people poorly.

In Matthew 25 Jesus said that when He returns, He will judge the nations based on their treatment of His brethren, the Jewish people:

All the nations will be gathered before Him, and He will separate them one from another, as a shepherd divides his sheep from the goats. And He will set the sheep on His right hand, but the goats on the left. Then the King will say to those on His right hand, "Come, you blessed of My Father, inherit the kingdom prepared for you from the foundation of the world: for I was hungry and you gave Me food; I was thirsty and you gave Me drink; I was a stranger and you took Me in; I was naked and you clothed Me; I was sick and you visited Me; I was in prison and you came to Me."

Then the righteous will answer Him, saying, "Lord, when did we see You hungry and feed You, or thirsty and give You drink? When did we see You a stranger and take You in, or naked and clothe You? Or when did we see You sick, or in prison, and come to You?" And the King will answer and say to them, "Assuredly, I say to you, inasmuch as you did it to one of the least of these My brethren, you did it to Me." (vv. 32–40)

In this passage, Jesus described gathering the nations before Him as "sheep and goats" and said that from His throne, He will judge *both* based on their treatment of His "brethren." He will bless the "sheep" nations that blessed Israel. But to the "goat" nations that did not bless His brethren He will say, "Depart from Me, you cursed, into the everlasting fire prepared for the devil and his angels" (v. 41).

Some Christians read this parable and apply it in a general sense to the needy or the poor. Yes, Jesus cares about the needy and the poor! But in context, Joel 3 and Matthew 25 indicate that judgment is coming to nations based on how they treated His brethren—the *children of Israel*. It is important to interpret Matthew 25 and the parable of the sheep and goats in the context of Jesus' Bible—the Old Testament—in which Joel and Zechariah had prophesied hundreds of years earlier. Judgment *is* coming to nations based on their treatment of God's people: Israel.

THE CALLING OF THE CHURCH

Israel has a clear call to bring the knowledge of God and the blessing of redemption to *all* humanity. Isaiah said the children of Israel are to be "a light to" the nations (49:6). But the church has a distinct calling too. Before unpacking what that calling is, let's define "church."

In our English Bibles, the word "church" is translated from the Greek word *ekklesia*, which means "a called-out assembly or congregation." The church is not a building but Jews and gentiles who confess Jesus as Lord and represent Him on the earth (Matthew 16:18; Ephesians 1:22; 1 Timothy 3:15).

Believers in Jesus are called to go out into the world and be a witness for Him. Various descriptions of that Great Commission are present in the New Testament, but Jesus' clearest instructions are in Matthew 28:19–20:

> Go therefore and *make disciples of all the nations*, baptizing them in the name of the Father and of the Son and of the Holy Spirit, *teaching them to observe all things that I have commanded you*; and lo, I am with you always, even to the end of the age. (Emphasis added)

Jesus instructed His followers to make disciples of all the nations. A disciple is someone who adheres to the teaching of another, a "follower" or "learner." This means Jesus' commission to the church is to make more followers of Him by teaching the nations to "observe all things" that Jesus commanded. We are to share the good news of Jesus' life, death, resurrection, and soon-coming return to a lost world. And we are to teach others to do the same.

More simply, we are to share the gospel.

The gospel is the good news of Jesus Christ—that by His blood shed on the cross, anyone who believes in Him can enter His kingdom *now*. But this "good news" is more than a present reality; God's kingdom on

Earth today is a mere shadow of the fullness of that kingdom when Jesus returns as King to rule and reign from Jerusalem:

> And this *gospel of the kingdom* will be preached in all the world as a witness to all the nations, and then the end will come. (Matthew 24:14, emphasis added)

This is the good news the church is to proclaim to the nations!

TWO COMPLEMENTARY CALLINGS

Though the nation of Israel and the church have different roles in God's plan of redemption, their roles complement each other. One might say they "complete" each other. Therefore, it is theologically incorrect to declare that God no longer works with the Jewish people or that the church has replaced the Jewish people as the people of God.

The calling on the church is *not* the same as the calling on the Jewish people—both "callings" are still in place and critical in God's redemptive plan. Israel's calling as God's birthing people and vehicle of His redemptive plan remains, as does the church's calling to make disciples among the nations.

We are to proclaim the gospel of our coming King and that when Jesus returns, He will come to a specific place (Jerusalem) to establish God's kingdom on Earth. *Israel will usher in that kingdom—and her King.* And when He comes, He will judge the nations based on their treatment of Israel.

God did not give this "role" to the gentile believers! It is unique to the Jewish people. This significant and unique calling is why we must stand with the Jewish people and the State of Israel. The enemy is opposed to the reestablishment of the Jewish State and will do everything he can to stop it. And therefore, Israel needs our prayers, support, and encouragement. We are to be watchmen on the walls of Jerusalem until God makes Jerusalem "a praise in the earth" (see Isaiah 62:6–7).

On that day, the kingdom of God will descend to Earth—the new Jerusalem will come down from heaven and be married to the old Jerusalem. Then those who remain from the nations will come up to Jerusalem to worship Him. Isaiah said that on that day, there will be no more war, and God's law will go forth out of Zion (Jerusalem):

> Many people shall come and say, "Come, and let us go up to the mountain of the LORD, to the house of the God of Jacob; He will teach us His ways, and we shall walk in His paths." For *out of Zion shall go forth the law*, and the word of the LORD from Jerusalem. (Isaiah 2:3, emphasis added)

On this glorious day, Israel, the church, and the nations will be as one, God's presence will once again dwell with man, and the Lord Himself will teach His people His Word from Zion.

CHAPTER SEVEN

The God of the Bible

*Bless the LORD, O my soul; and all that is within me,
bless His holy name! Bless the LORD, O my soul, and forget not all
His benefits: who forgives all your iniquities,
who heals all your diseases, who redeems your life from destruction,
who crowns you with lovingkindness and tender mercies,
who satisfies your mouth with good things,
so that your youth is renewed like the eagle's.
—Psalm 103:1–5*

One chapter in one book cannot begin to describe the God of the Bible, nor can it give an exhaustive theological treatment of who this sovereign creator of the universe is. So instead, my goal is to address a few misperceptions about God that keep us from understanding His greatness and the continuity of the Bible.

We have already discovered that the Old and New Testaments are one book telling one grand story. Now we will learn they are also about the same God. For some, that statement might come as a surprise: *of course, it is the same God!*

But not everyone is convinced of this. Skeptics seeking to deconstruct the Christian faith typically start with the Old Testament and then move on to the *God* of the Old Testament. They will try to paint the Old Testament as about law and judgment and the New Testament as about grace and forgiveness. Therefore, for them, the God of the Old Testament is angry and judgmental, while the God of the New Testament is loving and forgiving.

This could not be further from the truth and why this chapter is so important.

A COMMON THREAD

God's grace and mercy permeate the stories in the Old Testament and the New. Even the law demonstrates God's mercy in that He provided a sacrifice for the atonement of sin. God *wanted* to forgive His people, and He *wanted* them to approach Him to receive that forgiveness—but in the proper way.

After the Israelites entered the wilderness of Sinai, God began to reveal Himself to them. He had demonstrated His great love for them by freeing them from slavery and then, in the wilderness, tenderly cared for them, providing food and water.

God then proposed marriage to Israel, what we know as the Mosaic covenant. The Mosaic covenant is a covenant of love in which this loving God reveals His holiness and righteousness. He longs to live among His people, but first, they must agree to live a life of holiness in obedience to His commandments.

After making this covenant with Israel, note the people's response:

> Then he took the Book of the Covenant and read in the hearing of the people. And they said, "All that the LORD has said we will do, and be obedient." (Exodus 24:7; see also 19:8; cf. Ruth 3:5)

Israel agreed to the terms of this covenant, and God immediately told His people to build the tabernacle, giving detailed instructions (see Exodus

26), so that He could dwell in their midst.

Modern Christians tend to read God's law and get bogged down in the requirements. As such they miss the whole point, which God declares clearly in Deuteronomy 6:4–5:

> Hear, O Israel: The LORD our God, the LORD is one! You shall love the LORD your God with all your heart, with all your soul, and with all your strength.

Undergirding every "law" was God's love for His people and His desire that they would love Him in return—with all their heart, soul, and strength. Out of that love, obedience would flow, and the natural result would be blessing. They would "multiply greatly as the LORD God of your fathers has promised you— 'a land flowing with milk and honey'" (Deuteronomy 6:3).

For this reason, Wheaton College Professor Emeritus Samuel J. Schultz titled his book *Deuteronomy: The Gospel of Love*. Schultz contends that Deuteronomy is not the narrative of an angry God ruling over a frightened nation but rather that of a God who deeply loves His people.[11]

Perhaps this is why Jesus quoted the book of Deuteronomy more than any other book of the Torah. For example, when a teacher of the law asked Jesus what the most important commandment is, Jesus quoted Deuteronomy 6:4–5, known in Judaism as the Shema:

> Hear, O Israel, the Lord our God, the Lord is one. And you should love the Lord your God with all your heart, with all your soul, with all your mind, and with all your strength. (Mark 12:29–30)

Not only was the law infused with the loving relationship it established, but it exhibited God's mercy. As part of building the tabernacle, He

---

[11] Schultz, S. J., *Deuteronomy: The Gospel of Love*. (Moody Press), 1972.

instructed them also to construct the ark of the covenant—a wooden chest covered in pure gold with an ornate lid—a treasured artifact for the Israelites. Exodus describes the ark as containing the two stone tablets of the Ten Commandments, but the book of Hebrews also indicates it stored Aaron's rod and a pot of manna.

Above this ark was to be a "mercy seat," the place from where God would meet with His children:

> You shall make a mercy seat of pure gold; two and a half cubits shall be its length and a cubit and a half its width. ... And there I will meet with you, and I will speak with you from above the mercy seat, from between the two cherubim which are on the ark of the Testimony, about everything which I will give you in commandment to the children of Israel. (Exodus 25:17, 22)

Notice that God desired to meet with His people from a seat of *mercy*—not from a seat of *judgment*. Many passages throughout the Old Testament reveal that God's instruction to His people to meet with Him at the seat of mercy aligns perfectly with His character.

HOW GOD DESCRIBES HIMSELF

In Exodus 33 Moses asked to see God and know Him better as they began this journey together. The Lord responded by confirming His grace and compassion:

> I will make all My goodness pass before you, and I will proclaim the name of the LORD before you. I will be gracious to whom I will be gracious, and I will have compassion on whom I will have compassion. (Exodus 33:19)

The Lord not only passed by Moses but described Himself with these words:

The LORD, the LORD God, merciful and gracious, longsuffering, and abounding in goodness and truth, *keeping mercy for thousands*, forgiving iniquity and transgression and sin, by no means clearing the guilty, *visiting the iniquity of the fathers upon the children and the children's children to the third and the fourth generation.* (Exodus 34:6–7, emphasis added)

The Ark and the Mercy Seat by Henry Davenport Northrop, 1894 (source: commons.wikimedia.org)

The God of the Old Testament describes Himself as merciful and gracious, longsuffering, and abounding in goodness, truth, and mercy. His character forgives iniquity, transgression, and sin but is also just—it does not pardon unrepentant guilt.

MERCIFUL, BUT JUST

Exodus 34:7 may sound peculiar in the context of talking about a merciful and gracious God. What does "visiting the iniquity of the fathers upon the children and the children's children to the third and the fourth generation" mean?

Admittedly, this is a difficult passage. It's repeated several times in the Old Testament and can be hard to understand from our twenty-first-century individualistic mindset, yet it's important information we don't want to miss.

Deuteronomy 5:9 adds a clarification to this principal: "I, the LORD your God, am a jealous God, visiting the iniquity of the fathers upon the children to the third and fourth generations *of those who hate Me*." In that verse, God presents a contrast: for those who hate Him, He visits the iniquity of the fathers upon the children for generations, but for those who love and obey Him, He pours out mercy, tenderness, and graciousness.

Yes, there's judgment for the guilty, but there's no mercy without judgment. Mercy can't exist unless a person receives it in place of something. And mercy comes *in place of* judgment. God is merciful but just, and He extends both.

HOW DID THE ISRAELITES VIEW GOD?

If the God of Israel were as harsh and judgmental as some try to say He was, then the people of Israel would have known. They were the ones who fought many terrible battles and were exiled to foreign lands. How did *they* view the God who had allowed all these terrible calamities? Consider two of many examples in the Old Testament that help answer that question.

Jonah

Jonah was a prophet from the Northern Kingdom of Israel in about the eighth century BC. In Jonah 1–3 God instructed the prophet to go to Nineveh in Assyria—an evil, powerful kingdom—and proclaim judgment upon the city. Jonah didn't want to go because he knew God would not carry out His judgment if the people repented. Selfishly, Jonah wanted God to punish the Assyrians for their wickedness.

So instead of going northeast toward Nineveh, Jonah boarded a ship headed west to Tarshish, which was in the opposite direction from Nineveh and considered the end of the world in Jonah's day. But then troubles came. Jonah was thrown overboard and swallowed by a great fish.

Jonah prayed to God from the tomb of the fish. In his brokenness, he repented and learned a bit about God's mercy as the fish vomited him out on dry land. Jonah then obeyed God and went to Nineveh to preach what God had commanded of him. In response to Jonah's message, the Assyrians fasted and repented, and God indeed "relented from the disaster that He had said He would bring upon them" (3:10).

Jonah was angry that God decided not to destroy Nineveh. He left the city and made a shelter to sit under, and God caused a vine to grow over him for shade. Jonah said to God:

> Ah, LORD, was not this what I said when I was still in my country? Therefore I fled previously to Tarshish; for *I know that You are a gracious and merciful God, slow to anger and abundant in lovingkindness, One who relents from doing harm.* Therefore now, O LORD, please take my life from me, for it is better for me to die than to live! (Jonah 4:2–3, emphasis added)

Jonah knew God was gracious and merciful and would forgive his enemy, the Assyrians, if they repented.

Psalm 103

Indeed, Israel understood God's longsuffering, compassionate, and loving character. Consider the psalmist's description of God and His dealings with Israel in Psalm 103:

> The LORD is merciful and gracious, slow to anger, and abounding in mercy. He will not always strive with us, nor will He keep His anger forever. He has not dealt with us according to our sins, nor punished us according to our iniquities. For as the heavens are high above the earth, so great is His mercy toward those who fear Him. (vv. 8–11)

The Old Testament is packed with descriptions of God as full of mercy and forgiveness. Here are a few more passages:

> Blessed is he whose transgression is forgiven, whose sin is covered. Blessed is the man to whom the LORD does not impute iniquity, and in whose spirit there is no deceit. (Psalm 32:1–2)

> I have blotted out, like a thick cloud, your transgressions, and like a cloud, your sins. Return to Me, for I have redeemed you. (Isaiah 44:22)

> No more shall every man teach his neighbor, and every man his brother, saying, "Know the LORD," for they all shall know Me, from the least of them to the greatest of them, says the LORD. For I will forgive their iniquity, and their sin I will remember no more. (Jeremiah 31:34)

> To the Lord our God belong mercy and forgiveness, though we have rebelled against Him. (Daniel 9:9)

GOD'S CHARACTER IN THE NEW TESTAMENT

The New Testament is also full of God's love and forgiveness—and His judgment. The whole reason Jesus came to Earth was to die to pay the price (take on the judgment) for our sin.

Jesus often spoke of judgment. For example, in Luke 12:5, He said: "Fear Him who, after He has killed, has power to cast into hell; yes, I say to you, fear Him!" The author of Hebrews wrote something similar: "It is a fearful thing to fall into the hands of the living God" (10:31) and, in 12:29, referred to God as a "consuming fire."

All the authors of the Bible, Old and New Testament alike, agree that God's love and forgiveness and His judgment are two sides of the same coin. One cannot be separated from the other. But at the same time, God is not *all* love and forgiveness or *all* judgment.

Consider the example of parents. If someone were mistreating your child or a child you love and care for, you would likely be angry. If you didn't want punishment for the bully beating up your child every day at school, your love for your child would be questionable.

For people to experience God's love and forgiveness, judgment must also exist. It's the other side of the coin.

WHAT GOD IS AND IS NOT

We often put God in a box based on our culture, personality, likes, and dislikes. We want Him to be what we think is good and right so that we can *like* Him. However, we must remove God from that box because He is much greater than our limited understanding, which is based on our limited experiences. Let's stop defining God and allow Him to reveal Himself to us!

Not Limited by Culture

It is not easy to remove ourselves from our culture because, in many ways, we are products of that culture. For example, I grew up in a small southern town that emphasized good manners. We were to be kind and respectful to others. We were to exhibit those qualities in our talk, actions, and interactions with others. We addressed our elders with "yes, ma'am" and "yes, sir." We used proper etiquette at the dinner table. (The South had many spoken—and unspoken—rules!) My southern upbringing says God must always be kind, well-mannered, loving, and forgiving. He would never become angry or show emotion or punish someone!

Most of us don't like the thought of judgment, punishment, hell, or even war—so we try to keep those things out of the "God box." Instead, we need to take *God* out of that box. It is far too small and restricting.

Not Limited by Experience

Others put God in a box defined by past experiences and relationships. They relate to Him the way they relate to other authority figures in their life.

For example, people with wonderful, loving fathers tend to relate to God as a wonderful and loving father. People with abusive fathers or no father or who had a terrible childhood often don't know *how* to relate to God as merciful and loving. They never had a loving father and don't know how to relate to one. They expect God to be angry because that is how their authority figures were.

Others put God in a box based on how they see themselves. For example, people who have experienced rejection are often afraid God will reject them too. They feel God is always judging them and will never accept them. Our insecurities can create a barrier to appropriately relating to God. But He is not the problem—we are.

Then there are people with egos so big they cannot see their own faults, much less accept correction or rebuke. Their view of God is typically self-serving and validates their need for attention. They always need to be right, so their God affirms and blesses but never corrects.

Regardless of how we grew up or what our parents were like, our experiences do not limit who God is—He is who He is, whether we recognize it or not. But those experiences do limit our ability to get to know *all* of God—and to do that, we must throw away our boxes and ask God to reveal Himself to us.

Not Limited by Time and Space

The God of the Bible is not like us, but sometimes we view Him as a mere human. We think that since humans have certain limitations, God must too. One is time and space. Humans are limited to being in one place at one time. We can only see today, and there is no way to know what will happen the next day, next year, or next century. They can guess, but they can't truly know.

Unlike human beings, God is not limited to time and space. He already knows the end from the beginning (Isaiah 46:10). He sees all time at once and knows everything. Humans see today and can look back and see yesterday, but they can't see the beginning of time or the end.

Not Limited by Human Emotions

God is also not limited to human emotions. Humans can love one person one moment and be enraged at another the next, but they can't feel both love and anger simultaneously. God feels *everything* at once. His love and judgment are one. It's out of love that He judges sin, and it's out of justice that He loves mercy.

Not Limited by the People He Uses

God is sovereign, which means He has absolute power or controlling influence.[12] His sovereignty is most clearly seen in how He is perfectly executing His eternal plan to redeem humanity. He made unconditional promises to Abraham, Isaac, Jacob, and David. He will fulfill those promises no matter what anyone does or does not do. None of God's promises depended on people but only on Him—our sovereign God, who

---

[12] "Sovereignty," *Merriam-Webster Dictionary*, 2022.

has absolute control over the universe.

Throughout God's story, He has used men and women, despite their failures. For instance, He called David "a man after [His] own heart" (Acts 13:22; see also 1 Samuel 13:14), even though David committed adultery.

He also has worked through kingdoms, despite their evil intents. For example, He used Egypt to save the Jewish people from famine and sustain them, Assyria to execute judgment and exile Israel from their land, and Persia to send His people back to the land of Israel to rebuild. He even used Rome and the Roman census to move Mary and Joseph from Nazareth to Bethlehem for the birth of Jesus.

This is our great and sovereign God, who is above the affairs of the earth but busy at work in ordinary human beings' hearts and lives. He is not limited by anything we might think, say, or do—nothing that happens in this universe is outside His sovereignty.

HE IS THE GOD OF LOVE

The God of the Old Testament created man to have fellowship with Him in the garden. When man rebelled and disobeyed God, it broke His heart. From that point on, He wanted to bring man back into fellowship with Him. That is when he announced His plan to Abraham to produce a nation to be His vehicle for redeeming and blessing humankind. He created that nation and gave them a land as their inheritance. He revealed Himself to them and entered a marriage-like covenant of loving obedience and relationship.

Man, however, could not keep from sinning and fell deeper and deeper into it. Even after being exiled out of their land, God brought them back, and they rebuilt the temple and their national life. Then when the time was right, the Messiah was born. It was the loving God of the Old Testament who had prepared the world for Jesus' arrival over hundreds of years.

Jesus walked the earth, revealing the Father's loving heart to the children of Israel. He died a substitutionary death on the cross to pay for the sins of the world. All man had to do was believe in Him and receive forgiveness. For 2,000 years followers of Jesus have been proclaiming the good news of this forgiveness to a fallen and broken world.

The same God who defined right and wrong also determined consequences for doing right and doing wrong. He will uphold the standards He set. He will punish evil, and the unrepentant will suffer hell. But it is God's love and mercy that sent His only begotten Son to pay the price and open the way for us to experience the consequences of doing right—even though we failed.

The continuity of the story of the Bible is proof of the continuity of God. He is loving and merciful—and just.

SEEK THE LORD

To know this God of the Bible better, take a moment and tell Him. He has promised that if you seek Him, you will find Him:

> You will seek Me and find Me, when you search for Me with all your heart. (Jeremiah 29:13)

> Call to Me, and I will answer you, and show you great and mighty things, which you do not know. (Jeremiah 33:3)

Earnestly seek Him with all your heart. He will reveal Himself to you and destroy your limited "God box" for good!

CHAPTER EIGHT

The Search Begins

For the LORD gives wisdom;
from His mouth come knowledge and understanding.
—Proverbs 2:6

I hated history throughout high school and my early college years. I think it's because of the way it was taught. I mastered memorizing dates and events to pass a test but did not understand the context and overall significance of what I was reading.

All of that changed the moment I realized the Bible was a history book. That was the day I found a new interest in what had previously been a dreaded subject. And now, the more history I learn, the more exciting it is because I see the hand of God through it all.

I have come to realize that all of history is really *His*-story.

And as the God *of* history and the God *over* history, He is sovereign over all.

THE SOVEREIGN GOD WHO LOVES YOU

This sovereign God is weaving an amazing narrative over thousands of years, and it is all because of His great love for you. He chose one man to birth a nation through whom He would create a global family from every tribe and tongue. And He wants *you* to be part of it!

The nation God chose to use was not mythology but real people living in real places. Therefore, studying them in their historical and cultural context helps the characters and events come alive. So while you read your Bible for personal inspiration and engage in deeper, more doctrinal study, always be mindful of the historical context of what you are reading. That is when your Bible becomes so real it is as if it is three-dimensional.

And remember: *He did all of this to birth a family.* Israel was the vehicle through which God would reach the world. You and I can be part of His global family because of this grand scheme our sovereign God has weaved through all of history.

The apostle Paul said God planned all this before He created the world. He prepared the way—even predestined—for us to be adopted into God's family by Christ Jesus (Ephesians 1:3–6). John described this family in Revelation 7 as a multitude of souls no one can number from all nations, tribes, peoples, and tongues (v. 9). But to create this family, God had to start with one person—Abraham. From Abraham and his wife Sarah came descendants too numerous to count. These descendants are the Jewish people, the nation of Israel.

Yet God's ultimate goal was always a family made up of all of us—Jews and gentiles—through faith in Jesus:

> But as many as received Him, to them He gave the right to become children of God, to those who believe in His name: who were born, not of blood, nor of the will of the flesh, nor of the will of man, but of God. (John 1:12–13)

Paul compared the adoption of gentiles into the family of God to wild olive branches grafted into a natural olive tree:

> If some of the branches were broken off, and you [gentiles], being a wild olive tree, were grafted in among them, and with them became a partaker of the root and fatness of the olive tree, do not boast against the branches. But if you do boast, remember that you do not support the root, but the *root supports you*. (Romans 11:17–18, emphasis added)

A SOVEREIGN GOD WHO KEEPS HIS PROMISES

As the story of the Bible becomes clearer, you will more fully understand something key about God's character: He is faithful. And because "faithful" is *who God is*, you can trust Him. He cannot go back on His word:

> My covenant I will not break, nor alter the word that has gone out of My lips. (Psalm 89:34)

> God is not a man, that He should lie, nor a son of man, that He should repent. Has He said, and will He not do? Or has He spoken, and will He not make it good? (Numbers 23:19)

Once God has said or promised something, it's done. He does not break His promises, and He doesn't change what He said.

A good father never makes promises to his child only to renege on them. Similarly, God will not rescind His promises to Israel or us—adopted-in gentiles. On the contrary, because God is faithful and has kept (and will continue to keep) His word to Israel, we know He will fulfill His promises to *all* His children.

And He certainly made some amazing promises to the Jewish people. Yes, some of His promises were contingent upon them living in right relationship with Him. But there were other promises without conditions based purely on His ability and not anything man would or would not do.

He promised Abraham a great nation with a mission to bless the world. Included in that everlasting covenant was the land of Canaan as an everlasting possession. God promised the children of Israel that even if they were banished from the land due to sin, He would one day bring them back from every country they were scattered to. He also promised they would never cease being His people.

He promised King David an eternal kingdom. He declared through the prophets Isaiah and Zechariah that one day, even the nations of the world would come up to Jerusalem and worship Him, the One True God—*their* God. In other words, the nations would become part of His family and worship Him.

A SOVEREIGN GOD WHOSE TIMING IS PERFECT

The fact that God is currently working with both Israel and the church may be a new and somewhat confusing thought for some. It is not an easy concept to understand, which is why the apostle Paul called it a "mystery":

> For I do not desire, brethren, that you should be ignorant of this *mystery*, lest you should be wise in your own opinion, that blindness in part has happened to Israel until the fullness of the Gentiles has come in. And so all Israel will be saved, as it is written: "The Deliverer will come out of Zion, and He will turn away ungodliness from Jacob." (Romans 11:25–26, emphasis added)

This passage in Romans indicates there's a timing issue that only God knows. Paul said Israel is being kept until a certain time when the evangelizing work of the church has been completed. Then the Lord will turn to His people Israel and open their eyes to understand the depth of who He is and what He has done for them. Paul explained that this is what the Hebrew Scriptures promised.

I believe this is the day of national repentance the Hebrew prophet

Zechariah described so vividly:

> And I will pour on the house of David and on the inhabitants of Jerusalem the Spirit of grace and supplication; then they will look on Me whom they pierced. Yes, they will mourn for Him as one mourns for his only son, and grieve for Him as one grieves for a firstborn. In that day there shall be a great mourning in Jerusalem. (Zechariah 12:10–11)

As we await the final fulfillment of all God's promises, it may look like He's taking a long time finishing this story! But that is because we are filtering Scripture according to *our* time and not according to *heaven's clock*. The biblical narrative has been playing out for thousands of years. But since God lives outside our restrictions of time and space, He sees the end from the beginning. To us it looks like a long time, but God sees an entirely different reality.

THE BIBLE IS OUR ROADMAP

In the meantime, God has given us the Bible so we can better understand the times in which we live and His role for us as individuals and nations. The Bible is a road map for those who follow Jesus and want to understand God's plan, where He is revealing Himself today, and what is ahead. If we follow this road map, we will see how God has revealed Himself and His plan over time. As we progress through the story, we learn line upon line and layer upon layer about God, His ways, His intention, His relationship with His children, and who He is—His character and attributes.

Of course, the Bible will not answer every question (I often joke that God's probably going to keep me on Earth for as long as He can because He knows my list of questions is long, and I want to sit with Him and discuss every detail!). But the truth is, the more you know God, the less important those questions become. And I believe that once we enter eternity, those questions will evaporate.

The Bible is complete, and everything we need to know about God's plan is contained within its pages. Through His Spirit, He allows us to see and understand what we need to know today for the tasks at hand. We are finite human beings, so our understanding of our infinite God and His plan will always be limited this side of heaven.

The apostle Paul addressed this in 1 Corinthians 13:12, encouraging us that though we "see in a mirror, dimly" now, one day, we will see Jesus "face to face." Today we know "in part, but then [we] shall know just as [we] also [are] known."

Ultimately, reading and studying the Bible is about a relationship with the God of the universe. It's about spending time with Him, meditating on His Word, promises, and ways, and learning to discern His voice as He speaks to us while we do.

I was blessed to have had a spiritual father in my life who had been in ministry for 70 years when he passed away in his late 90s. I would visit him in his home and see his Bible on the kitchen table from his morning quiet time. When he was younger, he had a photographic memory and could quote most of the Bible by heart. His son told me that when he and his sisters were young, they would test their father's memory by calling out a Bible chapter and verse to see if he could quote it.

And he always could.

Yet that man started his day every morning in his Bible, reading and praying and highlighting and researching. Why? Because of his intimate relationship with God and what God would reveal to him through the Holy Spirit every time he combed through Scripture.

Reading and studying the Bible is certainly not just about increasing head knowledge. It is about relationship. The more we search God's Word, the more we will learn. And as the Bible makes more sense, our relationship with God will grow deeper.

He is waiting and ready to spend time with anyone who seeks after Him.

THE SEARCH BEGINS

GOD'S PROMISE TO YOU

King Solomon was known for building the First Temple—but Scripture also says that at the time, he was the wisest man who had ever lived. This great king offered wisdom that twenty-first-century believers would do well to heed:

> If you cry out for discernment, and lift up your voice for understanding, if you seek her as silver, and *search for her as for hidden treasures*; then you will understand the fear of the LORD, and find the knowledge of God. For the LORD gives wisdom; from His mouth come knowledge and understanding; He stores up sound wisdom for the upright; He is a shield to those who walk uprightly. (Proverbs 2:3–7, emphasis added)

God wants you to approach Him with your whole heart as if looking for a hidden treasure. And He promises that when you do, He will give knowledge and understanding.

Centuries later Jesus would say the same thing, using different words:

> So I say to you, ask, and it will be given to you; seek, and you will find; knock, and it will be opened to you. For everyone who asks receives, and he who seeks finds, and to him who knocks it will be opened. (Luke 11:9–10)

This is God's promise to you, and the Bible is your roadmap to a better understanding of Him and His ways. He is a faithful and true God, a loving Father to His family. He is not intimidated by your questions, so bring them along. The Bible will answer many of those questions, while others will remain a mystery. But your questions will fade in importance as you get to know Him better.

Seek God to know Him—His goodness, faithfulness, mercy, and

lovingkindness. Search His Word to understand His truth. You will find it.

YOUR NEXT STEP ...

Now that you are ready to begin reading the Bible for yourself, please turn to Appendix B for a list of resources to help you on your journey.

And the search begins!

— APPENDIX A —
Old Testament Timeline

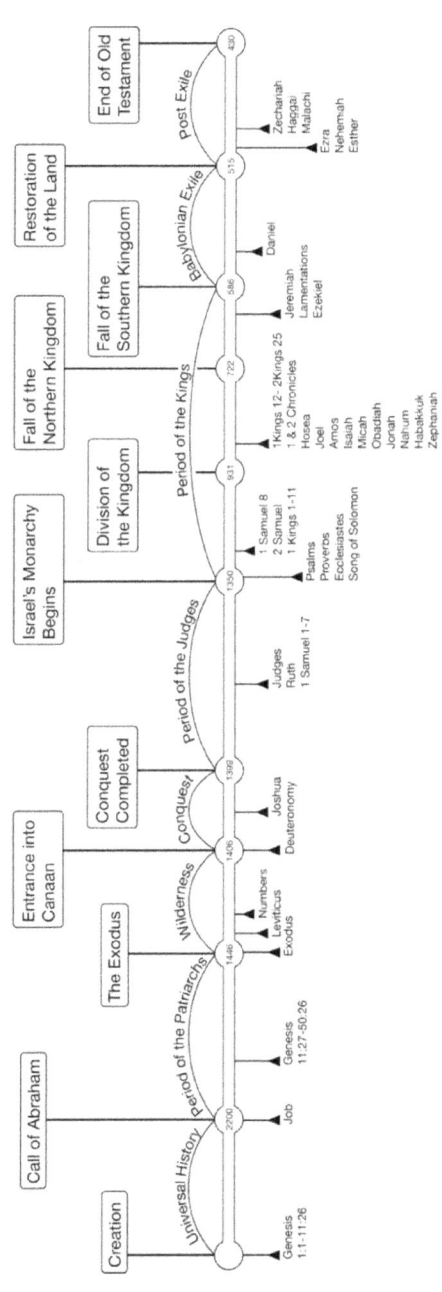

— APPENDIX B —
Recommended Resources

START READING YOUR BIBLE IN 3D TODAY!

The Daily Bible
by F. LaGard Smith

As this unique, chronological presentation of God's story daily unfolds before you, you will begin to appreciate God's plan for your life as never before. Reading the Bible will become a fresh, inviting, transformational experience. Available at the ICEJ USA store at: www.icejusa.org/product/the-daily-bible

"Walk Thru the Bible" Course (FREE)

Read through *The Daily Bible* by F. LaGard Smith, accompanied by Susan Michael's weekly teachings, and you'll cover the entire Bible in one year or at your own pace: www.iceju.org

Israel Study Tour

An Israel study tour will bring the Bible to life before your eyes and deepen your faith and relationship with God. The US Branch of the International Christian Embassy Jerusalem (ICEJ) offers various tours to Israel tailor-made for churches, young adults, pastors/leaders, and families, as well as our annual Feast of Tabernacles tour. Sign up here to be added to the ICEJ Israel tour list: www.icejusa.org/tours

ADDITIONAL RESOURCES

The Basis for Christian Support of Israel
by Malcolm Hedding

The Basis for Christian Support for Israel is an invaluable resource for pastors, Bible study leaders, and any Christian wanting to go deeper in their understanding of these powerful biblical truths and the days in which we live. Available at the ICEJ USA store at: www.icejusa.org/product/the-basis-of-christian-support-for-israel

The Great Covenants of the Bible
by Malcolm Hedding

This exciting study explains how the Abrahamic, Mosaic, new, and Davidic covenants are interrelated and vital in God's plan to redeem the world. In *The Great Covenants of the Bible*, you'll learn how Israel not only mediates these covenants for the world but why her calling is irrevocable, and her work is not yet finished. This study also exposes the error of Replacement Theology. Available at the ICEJ USA store at: www.icejusa.org/product/the-great-covenants-of-the-bible

How to Study Your Bible: Discover the Life-Changing Approach to God's Word
by Kay Arthur, David Arthur, and Pete De Lacy

In this dynamic guide to studying the Bible, bestselling author Kay Arthur invites readers of all levels of Bible literacy and learning to dive deeper into God's promises using the inductive Bible study method, also called the Precept method. This method cultivates the skills of observation, interpretation, and application and encourages readers to become active participants in God's Word. In 15 easy-to-understand chapters, the authors present a systematic approach that includes key words, context studies, comparisons and contrasts, topical studies, and more. It's a life-changing way of understanding and exploring Scripture that reveals the Bible's messages to readers and helps them live boldly and confidently in God's truths. Available on Amazon or through your favorite book retailer.

Israel Matters: Why Christians Must Think Differently about the People and the Land
by Gerald R. McDermott

Israel Matters addresses the perennially important issue of the relationship between Christianity and the people and land of Israel. McDermott challenges the widespread Christian assumption that since Jesus came to Earth, Jews are no longer special to God as a people and the land of Israel is no longer theologically significant. It traces the author's journey from thinking those things to discovering that the New Testament authors believed the opposite of both. It also shows that contrary to what many Christians believe, the church is not the new Israel, and both the people and the land of Israel are important to God and the future of redemption. Available on Amazon or through your favorite book retailer.

It Must Be Finished: Making Sense of the Return of Jesus
by Samuel Whitefield

In *It Must Be Finished*, Samuel Whitefield explains from beginning to end God's covenants, the tension between the Abrahamic covenant and the Mosaic covenant—and how that tension is resolved in the fulfillment of the new covenant. Available at the ICEJ USA store at: www.icejusa.org/product/it-must-be-finished

The New Inductive Study Bible
Precept Ministries International

This Bible, available in several different translations, is based entirely on the inductive study approach, leading readers directly back to the source and allowing God's Word to become its own commentary. It includes four full-color pages with step-by-step instructions for studying and marking the texts, more than 20 pages of full-color charts and maps, historical timelines, and dozens of unique study helps. Available on Amazon or through your favorite book retailer.

Our Father Abraham: The Jewish Roots of the Christian Faith
by Dr. Marvin Wilson

Although the roots of Christianity run deep into Hebrew soil, many Christians remain regrettably uninformed about the rich Jewish heritage of the church. *Our Father Abraham* delineates the vital link between Judaism and Christianity, exemplified by the common ancestry of the two faiths traceable back to Abraham. Marvin Wilson calls Christians to reexamine their Semitic heritage to regain a more authentically biblical understanding of what they believe and practice. Available at the ICEJ USA store at: www.icejusa.org/product/our-father-abraham

Thou Shalt Innovate
by Avi Jorisch

Though Shalt Innovate explores Israeli innovations that are collectively changing the lives of billions of people around the world and why Israeli innovators of all faiths feel compelled to make the world better. It's the story of how Israelis are helping to feed the hungry, cure the sick, protect the defenseless, and make the desert bloom by tapping into the nation's soul: the spirit of *tikkun olam*—the Jewish concept of repairing the world. Available at the ICEJ USA store at: www.icejusa.org/product/thoushaltinnovate

— GET YOUR FREE RESOURCE TODAY —

Request your FREE downloadable resource **Top 10 Finds in Israel That Support the Bible**—and share it with family and friends. This full-color resource includes vibrant pictures and maps of some of the top archaeological finds in Israel that support the biblical account. You'll also be alerted when we release a new book, online course, or other educational tools!

Get your free resource today by going to: www.icejusa.org/top10

— LEARN MORE ABOUT OTHER RESOURCES —
by Dr. Susan Michael at: www.susanmichael.com

— LEARN MORE ABOUT THE MINISTRY —
of the International Christian Embassy Jerusalem at: www.icejusa.org

— FOLLOW US ON —
f www.facebook.com/icejusa

www.instagram.com/icejusa_1980

— LEARN MORE ABOUT —
ICEJ U online courses, books, and podcasts at: www.iceju.org

— CONTACT US AT —
embassy.publishers@icejusa.org

ABOUT SUSAN MICHAEL

For more than 35 years, Susan has pioneered the development of the International Christian Embassy Jerusalem in the United States and around the world. She currently serves as the ministry's USA Director and is a member of the ICEJ's international Board of Directors. In addition to a master's degree in Judeo-Christian Studies from the Jerusalem University College, she holds a bachelor's degree in theology from Oral Roberts University and was awarded an Honorary Doctorate of Laws by Piedmont International University in 2018. Susan is an author, gifted teacher, and international speaker.

She is often called upon to address complex and sensitive issues such as antisemitism, Jewish-Christian relations, Christian Zionism, and current events in the Middle East to a diverse range of audiences. Her experience working with Jews, Christians, and Arabs from many national and denominational backgrounds has equipped her to handle delicate topics central to an understanding of Israel with extraordinary clarity and grace.

In recent years she has produced several educational tools to enable other Christians to do the same, including the ICEJ U online school, the IsraelAnswers.com website, biblical study tours to Israel through ICEJ USA Tours, and Susan's Blog of over 200 articles and podcasts. Susan has built the US Branch of the ICEJ into a scripturally sound, balanced, and reputable ministry, evidenced in its leadership of one of the strongest networks of Evangelical leaders in America—the American Christian Leaders for Israel (ACLI).

— ABOUT EMBASSY PUBLISHERS —

Embassy Publishers is the publishing arm of the International Christian Embassy Jerusalem designed to introduce the Christian reader to the biblical significance of Israel and the Jewish people, the history of antisemitism, Jewish-Christian relations, the modern State of Israel, and Christian engagement with Israel.

— ABOUT THE ICEJ —

The International Christian Embassy Jerusalem was established in 1980 in recognition of the biblical significance of all of Jerusalem and its unique connection with the Jewish people. Today, it represents millions of Christians, churches, and denominations to the nation and people of Israel. We recognize in the restoration of the State of Israel God's faithfulness to keep His ancient covenant with the Jewish people.

Our goal is to stand with Israel in support and friendship, equip and teach the worldwide church regarding God's purposes with Israel and the nations of the Middle East, be an active voice of reconciliation between Jews, Christians, and Arabs, and support the churches and congregations in the Holy Land. From its head offices in Jerusalem, the ICEJ reaches out to more than 170 countries worldwide, with branch offices and representation in over 90 nations.